Learning About Microbes: A Laboratory Manual

A Project of the Education Committee
of the Eastern Pennsylvania Branch of
The American Society for Microbiology

J. WESTON

WALCH

PUBLISHER

Portland, Maine

User's Guide
to
Walch Reproducible Books

As part of our general effort to provide educational materials that are as practical and economical as possible, we have designated this publication a "reproducible book." The designation means that the purchase of the book includes purchase of the right to limited reproduction of all pages on which this symbol appears:

Here is the basic Walch policy: We grant to individual purchasers of this book the right to make sufficient copies of reproducible pages for use by all students of a single teacher. This permission is limited to a single teacher and does not apply to entire schools or school systems, so institutions purchasing the book should pass the permission on to a single teacher. Copying of the book or its parts for resale is prohibited.

Any questions regarding this policy or requests to purchase further reproduction rights should be addressed to:

Permissions Editor
J. Weston Walch, Publisher
321 Valley Street • P.O. Box 658
Portland, Maine 04104-0658

1   2   3   4   5   6   7   8   9   10
ISBN 0-8251-3765-9
Copyright © 1998
J. Weston Walch, Publisher
P. O. Box 658 • Portland, Maine 04104-0658
Printed in the United States of America

Contents

Editorial and Contributory Staff

Senior Editor: Barbara B. McHale
Gwynedd-Mercy College, Gwynedd Valley, PA

Editors: Justine Baker
The Pennsylvania State University
Abington Campus, Abington, PA

RoseAnn Jakubowitch, Ph.D.
Sacred Heart Hospital, Allentown, PA

James Miller, Ph.D.
Delaware Valley College, Doylestown, PA

Barbara Morges

Contributors: Justine Baker
The Pennsylvania State University
Abington Campus, Abington, PA

Paul Cerwinka
Quest Diagnostics Incorporated
Horsham, PA

Conrad Kruse, Ph.D., *Retired*

Barbara B. McHale
Gwynedd-Mercy College, Gwynedd Valley, PA

James Miller, Ph.D.
Delaware Valley College, Doylestown, PA

Harriette Nadler, Ph.D.
Rhône Poulenc Rorer, Collegeville, PA

Josephine Smith, Ph.D., *Retired*

Norman Willett, Ph.D.
Temple University School of Medicine
Philadelphia, PA

Artist: Marcia Field

Introduction

This manual was written primarily to aid you, the high-school biology teacher, in teaching an important segment of the broad topic of biology. Middle-school and junior-high-school teachers will also find some of the exercises helpful in introducing the concept of the invisible life around us. College instructors may even find this information useful in classes designed for non-majors.

The format of the book is designed with your ease of use in mind: The time required for each experiment, as well as the appropriate grade level, are stated at the beginning of each exercise, allowing you to use only those exercises that are suitable for your students. Words that appear as key terms are boldfaced when first used in the text and experiments. A key term glossary is found in each chapter.

The exercises in this manual were designed with the constraints of the middle- or high-school biology laboratory in mind. Each procedure can be easily accomplished in a double lab period (In this manual, a period is equal to 45 minutes). For those situations in which only single periods are available, the theory can be presented during the first period, and the actual work performed during the next one. Although the exercises need not be done in order, and can be used individually and randomly, it is **extremely important that aseptic technique** (found on pages 1–14) **be introduced first** so that the microorganisms are safely and properly handled.

If you have never worked with microorganisms before, or if you have inadequate facilities for the proper execution of the exercises in which you are interested, please contact me at the following address for additional guidance:

Barbara McHale, Senior Editor
Gwynedd-Mercy College
Gwynedd Valley, PA 19437
(215) 641-5521

Safety Notes

Wear an apron . . . save a shirt.

Read techniques before beginning.

Properly record all observations.

Laboratory Safety Rules

1. Do not put any personal belongings, except your lab manual, on the lab bench during an experiment.

2. Do not bring food, drink, or cosmetics of any kind into the lab. This includes gum and hard candy.

3. If your hair is shoulder length or longer, you must keep it tied back while you are in the lab.

4. If you wear **soft** contact lenses, you MUST remove them before entering the lab; soft contact lenses absorb chemical fumes. If you wear **hard** contact lenses, you are strongly encouraged to remove them before the lab.

5. Wear lab aprons for all lab work.

6. Do not wear any clothing that could present a safety hazard: NO long, flowing sleeves; necklaces; etc.

7. Wash your hands with an antimicrobial soap every time you enter or leave the lab.

8. Clean the lab desk top with disinfectant at the beginning and end of each lab period.

9. NEVER place in your mouth any pencils, pens, labels, or other materials used during the lab.

10. Keep the lab workbench clear of flammables such as looseleaf paper and paper towels. Remove trash immediately and put it in the proper container.

11. Before lighting the Bunsen burner,

    (a) make sure that hose connections are tight.

    (b) know to which gas jet the burner is connected.

    (c) be sure that you are familiar with the correct, safe way to light the Bunsen burner.

12. If you are not using your Bunsen burner, keep it turned off!

13. NEVER take cultures from the laboratory.

14. Discard cultures only in biohazard containers. **Never discard cultures in the trash can!**

15. If a culture is spilled, notify the instructor immediately for proper cleanup procedures.

16. Handle microscopes with care! Use only lens paper to clean lenses.

17. ⚠ This symbol designates that **additional precautions** are necessary.

18. ☣ This is the international **biohazard symbol**—extra care needed!

Aseptic Technique

ASEPTIC TECHNIQUE

◆ Grade Level: 7–12, college
◆ Time Required for Experiment: two lab periods

The first period is a lecture covering the concepts of aseptic technique and the ubiquity of microorganisms. Concepts of sterilization are introduced as well as laboratory growth of microorganisms. Sterile media should be explained and examined. The second period consists of a demonstration by the teacher and the actual work done by the students.

To isolate bacteria from a single source (for example, soil), the sample is "streaked" on a plate of agar. Nutrient agar, a general-purpose medium that supports the growth of a wide variety of organisms, is often used. This streaking will help separate the different types of organisms; it results in continuous dilution of the initial sample to give well-separated surface colonies. After incubation, a small amount of material can be transferred from one colony and inoculated into a tube of broth, onto an agar slant, or onto another plate for maintenance of the culture. After incubation of this culture, the bacteria will be preserved longer if kept at about 5°C.

All materials used must be disposed of properly. All cultures, used culture media, glassware, disposable loops, and any other materials that have come in contact with bacteria must be sterilized in an autoclave at 15 pounds pressure and 121°C. If your school does not have access to an autoclave, call the senior editor of this book at the number listed on page vii for assistance.

For simplicity or for additional work, commercial yeast with a culture medium of Sabouraud Dextrose agar may be used.

NOTE: For each of the media inoculated, incubate one uninoculated tube or plate as a control at the proper temperature.

Answers to Questions

1. A pure culture contains organisms that are the same genus and species.

2. Microorganisms are "ubiquitous," meaning that they are everywhere—in air, in soil, and on and within living organisms.

3. Media and equipment must be sterilized to rid them of materials which would contaminate the pure culture.

4. Agar is a derivative of seaweed and is used as a hardening agent for microbiological media so that a solid surface is available for the growth of the organisms. It melts at 100°C and solidifies at 42°C to 45°C. It is neither liquefied at normal incubation temperatures nor attacked by most bacteria.

5. Most bacteria use the nutrients found in culture media. These consist of carbohydrates, proteins, minerals, vitamins, etc.

6. The medium prior to inoculation and incubation was clear (a slight yellow or tan color, but clear). If a sterile, uninoculated tube is incubated, none of the components precipitate and the tube remains clear.

7. Growth should be seen in all inoculated media. If growth was **NOT** seen, this could be caused by one of the following conditions:

   (a) The inoculating loop was not touched to the original culture.

   (b) The inoculating loop was too hot when touched to the original culture.

   (c) The incubation conditions were not suitable for the growth of the particular organism.

Key Terms

agar—seaweed-based hardening agent for culture media

algae—photosynthetic organisms with a defined nucleus that belong to the kingdom *Protista* or the kingdom *Plantae*

aseptic technique—method to keep out unwanted bacteria; also called **sterile technique**

autoclave—machine that generates steam pressure of 15 pounds per square inch; can reach temperatures of 121°C; and will kill even the most resistant forms of microorganisms

bacteria—unicellular organisms belonging to the kingdom *Monera* that have no organized nucleus (procaryotic cells)

broth—liquid medium used to support microbial growth

colonial morphology—form and structure of a colony of bacteria or fungi

colony—visible group of cells that have all formed from the division of one original cell

culture media—growth media for the cultivation of microorganisms

genus—"first name" of an organism according to the Linnaean system of classification, and representing organisms with similar characteristics

incubator—constant-temperature chamber used to grow microorganisms

microorganisms—organisms with single or few cells that can only be viewed using a microscope

mold—another name for "fungus"

petri dish—glass or plastic container used to grow microorganisms

protozoa—unicellular organisms with a defined nucleus that belong to the kingdom *Protista*

pure culture—culture of microorganisms that contains only one genus and one species

slant—culture medium containing agar that is allowed to harden at an angle

species—a closely related population of microorganisms; also the "second name" of an organism according to the Linnaean system of classification

sterile—free of living organisms

sterile technique—see **aseptic technique**

virus—submicroscopic, nonliving, parasitic, filterable agent consisting of a nucleic acid surrounded by a protein coat

yeast—unicellular fungus belonging to the class Ascomycetes

Aseptic Technique

INTRODUCTION

When **microorganisms** are found in nature, they usually exist with other microorganisms and not as a single **species**. For example, a pinch of soil or a drop of lake water will probably contain many types of **bacteria, viruses, yeast, molds, algae,** and **protozoa.**

When working with microorganisms in the laboratory, we need to work with one single species of organism. There are many ways to isolate or separate the various types of microorganisms to obtain what is called a **pure culture,** or a culture of only one **genus** and species of organism. These methods are called "pure culture techniques." When you try to isolate an organism, and also when the organism is growing as a pure culture, it is important that other organisms—from the air, your hands, the table—do not contaminate this culture. To make sure of this we use **aseptic** or **sterile technique** to handle microorganisms. Aseptic technique, or sterile technique, is the procedure designed to keep unwanted microorganisms from contaminating sterile materials or pure cultures of microorganisms. To facilitate this technique, all materials and media must be sterilized prior to use. Culture media and glassware are sterilized in an **autoclave** at 121°C, 15 pounds pressure, for about 15 minutes.

When bacteria or other microorganisms are grown in the laboratory, we need to provide nutrients—carbohydrates, proteins, vitamins, fats—to allow them to grow and reproduce. These nutrients are found in laboratory **culture media** and can be thought of as food for these organisms. The culture medium used can be a liquid called **broth** or a solid surface. The solid medium is simply broth to which **agar,** a hardening agent, has been added. Liquid agar poured into a test tube and allowed to harden at an angle is called a **slant.** Liquid agar poured into a **petri dish** provides a large surface on which organisms can grow.

Organisms also must be given oxygen (if they need it), the proper humidity, and a temperature similar to their natural habitat.

When bacteria grow on a solid surface, the number of cells increases until a visible mass of cells, called a **colony,** appears. Bacteria grow in different ways, and this difference in **colonial morphology,**

as it is called, helps us identify the type of bacteria. For example, some growth may be smooth or shiny, some even or jagged, and some may have different colors and textures. A variety of terms describe how organisms grow in a liquid and on solid surfaces. Use these terms to describe the results of the experiment that follows.

Characteristics of Bacterial Growth

Bacterial Colony Morphology

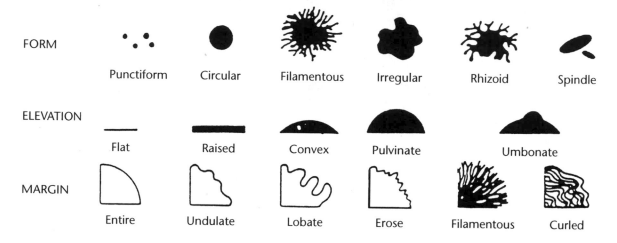

FORM

Punctiform Circular Filamentous Irregular Rhizoid Spindle

ELEVATION

Flat Raised Convex Pulvinate Umbonate

MARGIN

Entire Undulate Lobate Erose Filamentous Curled

Selected Features of Broth Culture

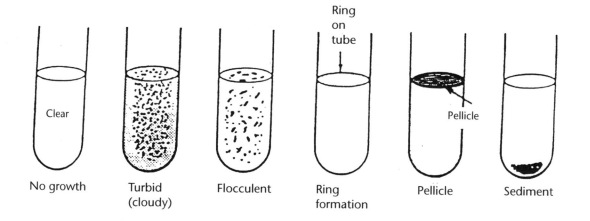

Ring on tube

Clear Pellicle

No growth Turbid (cloudy) Flocculent Ring formation Pellicle Sediment

NOTE: Several features may be found in one tube.

Objectives

1. Inoculate tubes of liquid media and slants.
2. Inoculate plated media to obtain isolated colonies of bacteria.
3. Recognize bacterial growth on plates, in broth, and on slants.
4. Demonstrate knowledge of, and consistently practice, aseptic technique.

Precautions

1. Always wear a disposable apron.
2. Wash your hands with an antimicrobial soap such as liquid Dial®.
3. Wipe tabletops thoroughly with Lysol®.
4. Be extremely careful when using the Bunsen burner.
5. Once the inoculating loop is sterilized, do not touch it to the table, your hands, or any other surface.
6. Do not leave lids open longer than necessary. (Do **NOT** put lids on the lab table.)
7. Never pick up test tubes by the lid.
8. Discard all materials in biohazard containers for proper disposal.
9. Autoclave **ALL** materials as soon as they are no longer needed.
10. Never discard cultures in the trash can.

Materials (Work individually.)

1. Plate cultures of:
   Escherichia coli
   Micrococcus luteus
   Rhodospirillum rubrum
   (A package of bakers' yeast can be substituted if bacterial cultures are unavailable.)
2. 1 **sterile** tube of Nutrient broth
   1 sterile slant of Nutrient agar
   1 sterile plate of Nutrient agar
3. Bunsen burner
4. Metal inoculating loop or sterile, plastic disposable loops
5. China marker
6. Test tube rack
7. Incubators—25°C and 37°C
8. Biohazard bag
9. Masking tape

Procedure

Pick one type of culture and use this culture to inoculate all three types of media.

A. Tube Transfer—Broth

1. Obtain a tube of sterile broth and mark on it the name of the organism you chose for your cultures, the date, and your initials.

2. Gripping the handle of the loop like a pencil, hold the loop in the Bunsen burner flame to sterilize the wire portion. Heat for at least 5 seconds after it glows red. (This step is unnecessary if a presterilized, disposable plastic loop is used.)

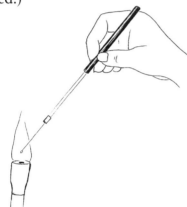

3. Allow the loop to cool for at least 5 seconds. **Do NOT** blow on it.

4. Open the plate culture like a clamshell and remove a small amount of growth using the *cooled* sterile loop. Close the lid.

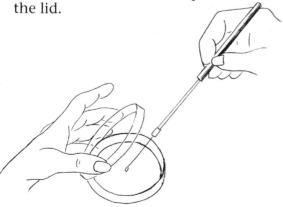

5. Remove the tube cap, holding it in the same hand as the loop. **Do NOT** place the cap on the table at any point.

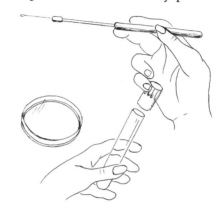

6. *Briefly* flame the mouth of the tube.

7. Dip the loop containing the culture into the broth and mix it to loosen the bacterial cells.

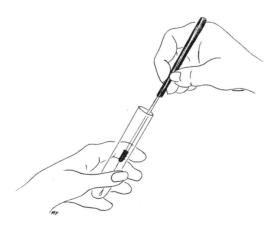

8. Flame the mouth of the tube, replace the cap, and place the tube back into the test tube rack.

9. Reflame the loop as in step 2 (unless disposable—then put into biohazard bag and autoclave or incinerate completely).

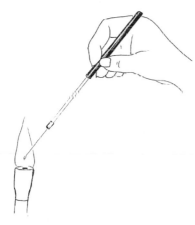

10. Incubate the *M. luteus* and *R. rubrum* at 25°C and the *E. coli* at 37°C.

B. Tube Transfer—Slant

1. Obtain a sterile slant and follow steps 1 through 6.

2. Inoculate the slant by placing the loop at the bottom of the slant and streak upward on the surface of the agar using a zigzag pattern.

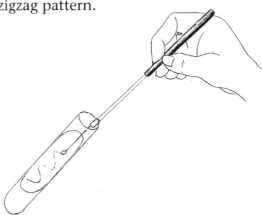

3. Follow steps 8 through 10.

C. Streak Plate

1. Turn the plate upside down and mark the bottom of the dish (the half that contains the agar) as shown in the diagram below.

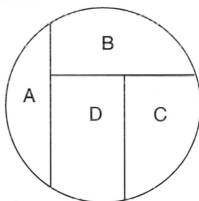

2. Also mark the bottom of the plate with the name of the organism, the date, and your initials.

3. Flame the loop in the Bunsen burner until it glows orange and then for at least 5 seconds more. (If presterilized, disposable plastic loops are used, a new one must be used for each step of this procedure.)

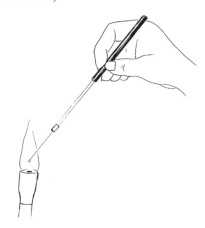

4. Allow the loop to cool for at least 5 seconds.

5. Open the culture plate like a clamshell and remove a small amount of growth. Close the lid.

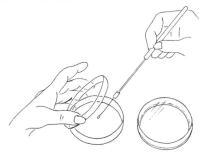

6. Open like a clamshell the sterile plate to be inoculated. Streak the loop back and forth in a zigzag pattern over area "A." Do NOT lift the loop from the agar and do NOT dig the agar surface. Close the lid.

7. Reflame the loop (unless disposable— then put into biohazard bag and auto-clave or incinerate completely).

8. While the loop is cooling, rotate the plate.

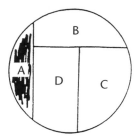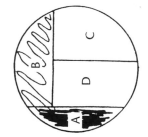

9. When the loop is cool, repeat steps 5 to 7 going into area "A" two or three times with the loop. Then streak area "B" using the same procedure as done in area "A." Close the lid.

10. Repeat this procedure of flaming and streaking until all sections of the plate have been streaked.

11. Reflame the loop.

12. Close the lid and tape it to the base of the plate, using two small pieces of tape. (To allow air to circulate, do not completely seal the opening between lid and base.)

13. Incubate the plate in the *inverted* position at the proper temperature for 48 hours.

NOTE: For each of the media inoculated, your teacher will incubate one uninoculated tube or plate at the proper temperature as a control.

Observations/Conclusions

NOTE: Use the uninoculated control tubes and plates for comparison with the inoculated materials.

1. Observe the broth tube for cloudiness indicating bacterial growth. Use the Characteristics of Bacterial Growth chart on page 6 to determine the growth pattern. The bottom of the tube may need to be tapped gently to resuspend the cells. Record the results in Table 1 of the Laboratory Report Form.

2. Examine the slant and the plate for growth and record the results in Table 1 of the Laboratory Report Form.

3. Complete Tables 2, 3, and 4 using the descriptive terms found in the chart on page 6.

Questions

1. What is meant by a pure culture?

2. Where are microorganisms found?

3. Why must all media and equipment be sterilized?

4. What is agar?

5. What do bacteria in these experiments use as food?

6. How do you know that cloudiness indicates bacterial growth?

7. Give two reasons why growth may not have occurred.

Key Terms

agar	microorganisms
algae	mold
aseptic technique	petri dish
autoclave	protozoa
bacteria	pure culture
broth	slant
colonial morphology	species
colony	sterile
culture media	sterile technique
genus	virus
incubator	yeast

streaking a plate

Suggested Readings

Kerr, T. J., and McHale, B. *Applications in General Microbiology*. 5th ed., Hunter Text-book, Winston-Salem, NC, 1998.

Seeley, H. W., VanDeMark, P. J., and Lee, J. J. *Microbes in Action*. W. H. Freeman, New York, NY, 1990.

Tortora, G. J., Funke, B. R., and Case, C. L. *Microbiology*. 6th ed., Benjamin Cummings, Menlo Park, CA, 1997.

Learning About Microbes

Microbiology Laboratory Report Form

Name _____ Date _____

+ = growth − = no growth

TABLE 1			
ORGANISM	BROTH	SLANT	PLATE
Escherichia coli			
Micrococcus luteus			
Rhodospirillum rubrum			
Control			

TABLE 2	
ORGANISM	DESCRIPTION OF GROWTH IN BROTH
Escherichia coli	
Micrococcus luteus	
Rhodospirillum rubrum	

TABLE 3	
ORGANISM	**DESCRIPTION OF GROWTH ON SLANT**
Escherichia coli	
Micrococcus luteus	
Rhodospirillum rubrum	

TABLE 4	
ORGANISM	**DESCRIPTION OF GROWTH ON PLATE**
Escherichia coli	
Micrococcus luteus	
Rhodospirillum rubrum	

Seeing Microorganisms

SEEING MICROORGANISMS: USE OF THE MICROSCOPE

◆ Grade Level: 8–12
◆ Time Required for Experiment: one to two class periods

Materials

Microscopes: Some microscopes are equipped with four objective lenses, some with two or three. This exercise has been written without specifying which low-power lenses are available. Assess the objective lens situation on your microscopes before addressing the class. You *will* need the oil immersion objective for this exercise.

Slides and coverslips: Slides and coverslips may be washed and used again. Plastic coverslips are acceptable.

Immersion oil: The refractive index of the immersion oil must match the refractive index of the glass in the lenses. The manufacturer of the microscope will specify which oil to buy. A mixture of Types A and B is often suitable for the classroom.

Water samples containing protozoa and algae: Pond water, aquarium water, or hay infusions may be used. Look at the samples ahead of time to be sure they contain an active population of microbes. If the population is not impressive, it can be augmented by adding a handful of grass or crumbled leaves and letting the mixture stand for a few days at room temperature.

Prepared slides of bacteria: Prepared slides that include the three basic shapes of bacteria—rods, cocci, and spirals—can be purchased from any of the biological educator's supply houses. See the Appendix for a list of suppliers.

Answers to Questions

1. and 2.

Ocular Lens	Objective Lens		Total Magnification
10X	scanning	4X	40X
10X	low power	10X	100X
10X	high dry power	40–50X*	400X–500X
10X	oil immersion	100X	1000X

*varies with manufacturer

3. Protozoa vary in size, but most are between 10 and 50 micrometers in diameter. (For comparison, the diameter of a human red blood cell is about 8 micrometers.)

4. Most bacteria are between 1 and 2 micrometers in length or diameter. A protozoan cell is thus generally 5 to 50 times larger than a bacterial cell.

Key Terms

algae—photosynthetic organisms with a defined nucleus that belong to the kingdom *Protista* or the kingdom *Plantae*

coarse adjustment knob—knob located on the side of the microscope that rapidly brings a specimen into focus

compound microscope—instrument that makes use of multiple lenses to increase the apparent size of an object.

coverslip—small piece of thin glass or plastic used on a microscope slide to cover the specimen

fine adjustment knob—small knob on the side of the microscope that slowly brings the specimen into fine focus

high dry lens—objective lens that has a magnification between 40X and 50X and is used to view algae, protozoa, and some very large bacteria

image—reproduction or likeness of an object

immersion oil—oil that has approximately the same refractive index (measurement of the deflection from a straight path undergone by a light ray in passing from one medium, such as air, into another) as glass (1.56)

low power lens—objective lens that usually has a magnification of 10X and is used to view algae, protozoa, and the arrangement of the specimen

objective lenses—lenses attached to the nosepiece of the microscope; the second in the series of lenses in a compound microscope

ocular lens—lens closest to the eye that usually has a magnification of 10X; the first in the series of lenses in a compound microscope

oil immersion lens—most powerful of the objective lenses and, with oil, is used to view bacteria; usually has a magnification of 100X

protozoa—unicellular organisms with a defined nucleus that belong to the kingdom *Protista*

stage—flat area of the microscope that holds the microscope slide

wet mount—placement of a drop of a liquid containing microorganisms on a microscope slide; a coverslip is placed on top of the drop to protect the microscope lenses from damage

Seeing Microorganisms: Use of the Microscope

INTRODUCTION

Most microbes are so small that they cannot be seen without the aid of the microscope. For this reason, the science of microbiology did not develop until the microscope was developed in the 1700's.

When you look at a microbe through the microscope, the **image** of the microbe is enlarged enough for you to see it. The magnification is accomplished by a series of glass lenses. Each lens by itself is similar to a hand-held magnifying glass, but the microscope is constructed so that we are actually looking through more than one lens at a time. The image magnified by one lens is further magnified by each succeeding lens so that we see a greatly enlarged image of the microbe. A microscope using more than one lens is called a **compound microscope**.

The lens at the top of the microscope, the one you look into, is the **ocular lens**. Its magnifying power is tenfold, or "10X." On the nosepiece of the microscope, above the **stage** on which the slide rests, there are three or four **objective lenses**. Only one of these is used at a time. It is best to start looking at a specimen with one of the smaller lenses, usually the **low power**, or 10X, objective lens and then move up gradually to the higher power objectives. Once the subject is in focus, rotate the nosepiece to bring the **high dry lens** (with magnifying power between 40X and 50X) into position. After the image has been refocused using the **fine adjustment knob**, place a drop of **immersion oil** directly on the material being examined. Then rotate the longest of the lenses, the **oil immersion lens**, into place and using the fine adjustment knob, adjust the focus a final time. Do not place any other lenses in the oil.

Immersion oil is a special kind of oil through which light passes the same way it passes through glass. It must be used with the oil immersion lens to get a sharp image. Do not be concerned if the tip of the oil immersion objective lens gets into the oil; it is supposed to! You will need to remove all of the oil with a piece of lens paper at the end of your microscope session. A commercial glass cleaner such as Windex® is helpful in dissolving the oil. Make sure to dry the lens with lens paper when finished and remove any oil that is on the stage as well.

Optical and mechanical features of the microscope

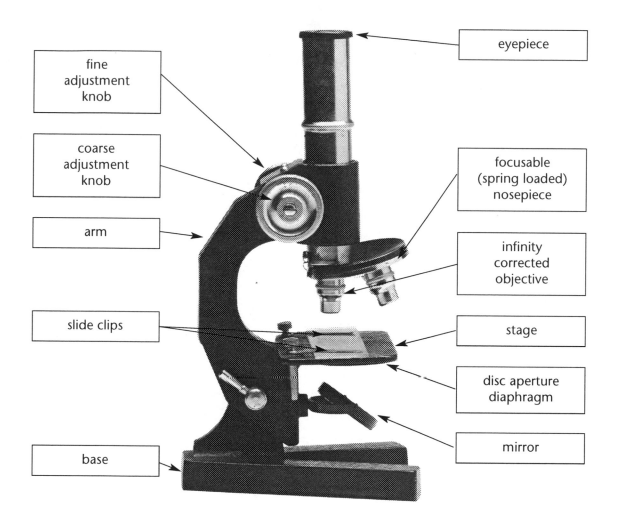

fine adjustment knob

coarse adjustment knob

arm

slide clips

base

eyepiece

focusable (spring loaded) nosepiece

infinity corrected objective

stage

disc aperture diaphragm

mirror

Objectives

1. Identify the parts of the microscope.
2. Learn how to use the compound microscope.
3. Observe various kinds of microorganisms.

Precautions

1. Use two hands to carry or move the microscope.

Materials

1. Microscopes, microscope slides, and coverslips
2. Prepared slides of bacteria
3. Water samples containing protozoa and algae (pond water, aquarium water, or hay infusion)
4. Immersion oil
5. Lens paper
6. Glass cleaner

Procedure

A. Observation of living protozoa and algae

NOTE: The oil immersion lens will not be used.

1. Place one drop of a water sample on a glass microscope slide.
2. Gently put a **coverslip** on the drop to prepare a **wet mount**.
3. Put the slide on the microscope stage and rotate the shortest objective lens into place.
4. Look through the ocular lens and, using the coarse and fine adjustment knobs, bring the specimen into focus. At this magnification you will not see the microbes yet, but you will be able to tell that you are at least focusing on the drop of water.
5. Rotate the nosepiece to the next higher power lens and refocus using the fine adjustment knob. When you get to the high dry lens with a magnification (by itself) of about 50X, do not forget that you are also looking through the ocular lens (10X). Thus the image of whatever you are looking at has been magnified a total of 500 times.
6. On Table 1 of the Laboratory Report Form, record or draw the organisms you see in the water sample. The rapidly swimming cells are **protozoa**; the green cells are **algae**.

    *Learning About Microbes*

B. Observation of bacteria on prepared slides

NOTE: Oil immersion lens will be used.

1. Obtain a prepared slide with stained bacteria and put it on the stage of your microscope. Do not use a coverslip.

2. As in Procedure A, start with the lowest power available and work up to higher magnifications. Bring the slide into focus with the high power dry lens. At this magnification you can see the bacteria but not in clear focus.

3. Rotate the nosepiece to move the lens out of the way and put *one drop* of immersion oil *directly* on the coverslip of the slide.

4. Bring the oil immersion lens into position. It will be immersed in the oil on the slide. Refocus the image with the fine adjustment knob. The combined magnifications of the two lenses (the 10X ocular and the 100X oil immersion lens) is 1,000X.

5. On Table 2 of the Laboratory Report Form, make drawings of the bacteria you see.

6. When you have finished with the microscope, wipe the oil from the lenses with a piece of lens paper moistened with a commercial glass cleaner. Dry the lens with another piece of lens paper.

Questions

1. What is the magnifying power of each of the lenses on the nosepiece of your microscope?

2. The magnifying power of the ocular lens is 10X. What is the *total magnification* when each of the objective lenses on the nosepiece is used?

3. Approximately how large is a protozoan cell?

4. How large is a bacterial cell? How does its size compare to the protozoan cell?

Key Terms

algae
coarse adjustment knob
compound microscope
coverslip
fine adjustment knob
high dry lens
image
immersion oil

low power lens
objective lenses
ocular lens
oil immersion lens
protozoa
stage
wet mount

Suggested Readings

Kerr, T. J., and McHale, B. *Applications in General Microbiology*. 5th ed., Hunter Text-book, Winston-Salem, NC, 1998.

Seeley, H.W., VanDeMark, P. J., and Lee, J. J. *Microbes In Action*. W.H. Freeman, New York, NY, 1990.

Tortora, G. J., Funke, B. R., and Case, C. L. *Microbiology*. 6th ed., Benjamin Cummings, Menlo Park, CA, 1997.

Learning About Microbes

Microbiology Laboratory Report Form

Name _____ Date _____

A. Observation of living protozoa and algae

TABLE 1	
ORGANISM	DRAWING

B. Observation of bacteria on prepared slides

TABLE 2	
NAME OF SLIDE USED	DRAWING

SEEING MICROORGANISMS: LEARNING ABOUT SIZE, SHAPE, AND ARRANGEMENT

◆ **Grade Level:** 7–12, college
◆ **Time Required for Experiment:** two lab periods

THE FAR SIDE By GARY LARSON

Early microbiologists

The first period is a lecture covering the concepts of bacterial morphology, including the differences between colonial and cellular morphology. The variety of sizes, shapes, and arrangements of bacteria are explained. The purpose of staining is introduced. The second period consists of a demonstration by the teacher and the actual staining done by the students.

EXPERIMENT 1

Answers to Questions

1. and 2.
   Students should see three different shapes of bacteria: *Escherichia coli* is rod-shaped and usually occurs singly; *Micrococcus luteus* is a coccus and usually occurs in clusters of eight cells; *Rhodospirillum rubrum* is curved or spiral-shaped and usually occurs singly.

3. Because bacteria are so small and colorless, staining is needed to provide contrast with the light background.

EXPERIMENT 2

NOTE: *Bacillus subtilis* and *Micrococcus luteus* are gram-positive; *Escherichia coli* and *Rhodospirillum rubrum* are gram-negative.

Answers to Questions

1. A differential staining procedure allows differentiation of cells based on cell wall components and is helpful in the identification of bacteria. A differential stain also shows the relative size, shape, and arrangement of bacteria.

2. Gram's (Lugol's) iodine is used as a mordant and increases the affinity of the cells for the primary dye, Gram's crystal violet.

3. Smears are heat-fixed to kill the cells and to cause them to adhere to the slide so that they do not wash off during the staining procedure.

4. The Gram stain can help you identify bacteria because it is based on the chemical composition of the bacterial cell wall. Bacteria that have high concentrations of peptidoglycan in their cell walls retain the primary dye and remain purple after decolorization with the alcohol. Bacteria that have high lipid concentrations in their cell walls do not retain the primary dye, but do take up the counterstain, Safranin, and appear pink or red.

Step	Reagent	Time	Gram +	Gram -
Primary dye	Crystal violet	1 min	purple	purple
Mordant	Gram's (Lugol's) iodine	1 min	purple	purple
Decolorizer	Ethyl alcohol	≤15 sec	purple	clear
Counterstain	Safranin	2 min	purple	red or pink

Key Terms

bacillus—any rod-shaped or oblong bacterium; when capitalized to refer to a genus, it refers to rod-shaped, endospore-forming, facultatively anaerobic, gram-positive bacteria

cellular morphology—form and structure of an individual cell

coccus—a spherical or ovoid bacterium

colonial morphology—form and structure of a colony of bacteria or fungi

counterstain—a stain used to give contrast in a differential staining procedure

decolorizer—a solution used in the process of removing a stain

differential staining—a staining process that distinguishes objects on the basis of reactions to the staining procedure

diplobacilli—rods that divide and remain attached in pairs

diplococci—cocci that divide and remain attached in pairs

Gram stain—a differential stain that divides bacteria into two groups: gram-positive and gram-negative

mordant—a substance added to a staining solution that makes it stain more intensely

morphology—the external appearance without regard to function

primary dye—the first dye used in a differential staining procedure

spirillum—a helical or corkscrew-shaped bacterium; when capitalized to refer to a genus, it refers to aerobic, helical bacteria with clumps or polar flagella

staphylococci—a grape-like cluster or broad sheet of spherical cocci

streptobacilli—rods that remain attached in chains after cell division

streptococci—a family of gram-positive cocci whose cells occur as pairs or chains, exhibiting facultatively anaerobic fermentative metabolism

Seeing Microorganisms: Learning About Size, Shape, and Arrangement

INTRODUCTION

The term **morphology** refers to the size and shape of an organism regardless of its function. **Colonial morphology** refers to the appearance of bacteria when they grow on a solid surface, and this growth can usually be seen with the naked eye. The terms used to describe the variety of appearances on a solid surface are described on page 6 in the Aseptic Technique lab. **Cellular morphology** refers to the size, shape, and arrangement of individual bacterial cells. These characteristics can only be determined using a microscope.

Most bacterial cells fall into one of the following categories:

round; called a **coccus** (cocci is plural);

rod-shaped; called a **bacillus** (bacilli is plural);

or curved; called a **spirillum** (spirilla is plural).

Some bacteria group together in a particular arrangement. This grouping can help to identify the bacteria.

Cocci can be in:

pairs
(diplococci)

chains
(streptococci)

clusters
(staphylococci)

Bacilli can be in:

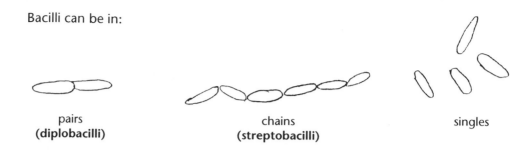

| pairs
(diplobacilli) | chains
(streptobacilli) | singles |

Spirilla are usually single cells, but can be:

| curved | spiral-shaped |

EXPERIMENT 1: SIMPLE STAINING

In nature, bacteria are usually very small and colorless, making them difficult to see, even with the light microscope. To view these micro-organisms, we stain them with a dye that is absorbed by the cell. Bacterial cells differ chemically from their surroundings and thus can be stained to contrast with their environment. Simple staining uses one dye to stain the cells, which allows you to see the relative size, shape, and arrangement of the microorganisms.

Objectives

1. Understand the difference between colonial and cellular morphology.
2. Prepare a smear of bacteria.
3. Perform a simple stain procedure.

Materials (Work individually.)

1. Plate cultures of: *Escherichia coli, Micrococcus luteus, Rhodospirillum rubrum*
2. Gram's crystal violet
3. Gram's safranine
4. Methylene blue
5. Glass microscope slides (3)
6. China marker

Learning About Microbes

7. Metal inoculating loop or sterile, plastic disposable loops
8. Bunsen burner
9. Bibulous paper to blot slides
10. Dish detergent
11. Paper towels
12. Immersion oil
13. Staining rack
14. Biohazard bag

Procedure

A. Preparation of Bacterial Smear

1. Clean the microscope slides with dish detergent such as Dawn®, rinse them thoroughly with tap water, and dry them with a paper towel.
2. Using a china marker, mark a slide with the name of the organism (*E. coli*), the date, and a circle in the center indicating where the bacteria will be placed.
3. Turn the slide over so that markings are on the *underside*.
4. Apply one loopful of water to the slide over the circle.
5. Using aseptic technique, apply a *small* amount of *E. coli* and mix with the loopful of water.
6. Spread into a thin film.
7. Allow the slide to air dry.
8. With the bacteria on the top side of the slide, heat-fix the slide by passing it, right-side up, through the Bunsen burner flame three times.
9. Repeat steps 2 to 8 for *M. luteus* and *R. rubrum*.

B. Staining Process

1. Allow the slides to cool before placing them on the staining rack over the sink.
2. Pour the Gram's crystal violet over the *E. coli* slide and allow it to stay on the slide for 1 minute.
3. Holding the slide at an angle, rinse it thoroughly with water until no more dye comes off the slide.
4. Using the bibulous paper, gently blot the slide until it is dry.
5. Pour the Gram's safranine over the *M. luteus* slide for 2 minutes.
6. Repeat steps 3 to 4.

Learning About Microbes

7. Pour the methylene blue over the *R. rubrum* slide for 2 minutes.

8. Repeat steps 3 to 4.

9. Apply one drop of immersion oil to each slide, and using the procedure described in the Use of the Microscope lab, observe the slides using the oil immersion lens.

10. When finished, gently blot the oil from your slide using a paper towel. Do not rub! Slides can be stored in a microscope slide box.

Observations/Conclusions

1. Record results in Table 1 of the Laboratory Report Form.

2. Were all the cells the same size?

3. Were some cells easier to see than others?

Questions

1. How many different shapes of bacteria did you see?

2. Name the different arrangements of bacteria that you saw.

3. Why did you need to stain the bacteria?

EXPERIMENT 2: DIFFERENTIAL STAINING

Microorganisms differ from one another chemically and physically and therefore may react differently to the same staining procedure. This is the basic principle of **differential staining**, a method of distinguishing between types of bacteria based on the chemical composition of their cell walls. The most important differential staining procedure is the **Gram stain**, first developed by Christian Gram over 100 years ago.

The Gram differentiation is based upon the application of four chemical reagents: **primary dye, mordant, decolorizer,** and **counterstain.** The primary dye, crystal violet, imparts a purple color to all organisms. Gram's (Lugol's) iodine then acts as a mordant, enhancing the union between the crystal violet dye and the cell to form a complex. The decolorizing solution of alcohol extracts the purple complex from certain cells more readily than others. A safranine counterstain colors those organisms that lost the purple complex. Those organisms retaining the purple complex are gram-positive (purple), while those losing it are gram-negative (pink or red).

Objectives

1. Understand the concept of differential staining.
2. Learn a differential staining technique that divides bacteria into two different groups and aids in their identification.
3. Successfully perform a Gram stain.

Materials

1. Plate cultures of *Bacillus subtillis, Escherichia coli, Micrococcus luteus, Rhodospirillum rubrum*
2. Gram's crystal violet
3. Gram's iodine
4. Ethyl alcohol
5. Gram's safranine
6. Glass microscope slides (4)
7. China marker
8. Metal inoculating loop or sterile, plastic disposable loops
9. Bunsen burner
10. Bibulous paper to blot slides

Learning About Microbes

11. Staining rack
12. Immersion oil
13. Paper towels
14. Dish detergent
15. Biohazard bag

Procedure

1. Prepare bacterial smears of the four different bacteria as described in Experiment 1, Part A.
2. Place the first slide on the staining rack.
3. Apply Gram's crystal violet and allow it to react for 1 minute.
4. Holding the slide at an angle, rinse it thoroughly with water until no more dye comes off the slide.
5. Flood the slide with Gram's iodine an allow it to react for 1 minute.
6. Rinse the slide as in step 4.
7. Holding the slide at an angle, carefully add the ethyl alcohol one drop at a time. As soon as color stops coming off the slide (after about 8 to 10 seconds), rinse with water to stop the decolorizing action.
8. Flood the slide with Gram's safranine and allow it to react for 2 minutes.
9. Drain the excess stain from the slide and rinse it.
10. Gently blot the stained slide using bibulous paper.
11. Repeat steps 3 to 10 for the other three slides.
12. Examine each slide under the microscope using the oil immersion objective.
13. When finished, gently blot the oil from your slide using a paper towel. Slides can be stored in a microscope slide box.

Observations/Conclusions

1. Record results in Table 2 on the Laboratory Report Form.
2. Were all the cells the same color?
3. Were some cells easier to see than others?

Learning About Microbes

Questions

1. What is the purpose of a differential staining procedure?

2. What is the purpose of Gram's iodine?

3. Why are the smears heat-fixed?

4. How can the Gram stain help you identify bacteria?

Key Terms

bacillus
cellular morphology
coccus
colonial morphology
counterstain
decolorizer
differential staining
diplobacilli
diplococci

Gram stain
mordant
morphology
primary dye
spirillum
staphylococci
streptobacilli
streptococci

Suggested Readings

Kerr, T. J., and McHale, B. *Applications in General Microbiology.* 5th ed., Hunter Textbook, Winston-Salem, NC, 1998.

Prescott, L. M., Harley, J. P., and Klein, D. A. *Microbiology.* William C. Brown, Dubuque, IA, 1990.

Tortora, G. J., Funke, B. R., and Case, C. L. *Microbiology—An Introduction.* 6th ed., Benjamin Cummings, Menlo Park, CA, 1997.

Wistreich, G. A., and Lechtman, M. D. *Microbiology.* 5th ed., Macmillan, New York, NY, 1984.

Microbiology Laboratory Report Form

Name _____ Date _____

Experiment 1: Simple stain

TABLE 1			
ORGANISM	SHAPE OF CELL	ARRANGEMENT OF CELL	DRAWING OF CELL
Escherichia coli			
Micrococcus luteus			
Rhodospirillum rubrum			

Experiment 2: Gram stain

TABLE 2			
ORGANISM	SHAPE OF CELL	COLOR OF CELL	GRAM REACTION
Bacillus subtilis			
Escherichia coli			
Micrococcus luteus			
Rhodospirillum rubrum			

Microbes in Everyday Life

MICROBES IN EVERYDAY LIFE: THE MICROBIOLOGY PICNIC

◆ Grade Level: 7–12
◆ Time Required for Experiment: one class period for preparatory discussion; one class period for laboratory (the picnic)

This is an easily performed class project and gives everyone a chance to be directly involved in the action. It requires some advance planning and some discussion about how microbes are involved in food preparation, but the actual lab is very simple.

Precautions

Many of the food items brought to the picnic will require refrigeration if they are to be stored longer than an hour before use. Many foods, if left at room temperature, can support growth of microbial populations, which can spoil food and possibly cause human illness. With proper precautions and common sense, there should be no threat to health involved with this project.

Answers to Questions

1. As yeast cells grow and divide, they produce carbon dioxide gas. This gas is trapped by the dough, making the dough expand.
2. Fermentation is a process by which some microbes derive energy from sugars. Acids or alcohols are formed as by-products of fermentation.
3. Foods provide nutrition for microbes as well as humans. If certain foods are exposed to warm temperatures, the few organisms that are present in harmless levels in all foods will multiply rapidly. The number of cells could reach dangerously high levels. If foods are not properly refrigerated, some organisms can also produce poisonous materials called toxins.

4. Many useful bacteria produce acids such as acetic acid or lactic acid. If litmus paper is available, you might test some of the foods. These acids are not harmful at the levels produced in foods, but they do enhance the flavors.

Key Terms

bacteria—unicellular organisms belonging to the kingdom *Monera* that have no organized nucleus (procaryotic cells)

fermentation—the breakdown of complex molecules such as sugar into organic compounds

microbes—any of the bacteria, protozoa, viruses, fungi, or algae

refrigeration—method used for the preservation of food by storage at 5°C. Low temperatures restrict rates of growth and enzyme activity.

yeast—unicellular fungi belonging to the class Ascomycetes

COMPOSTING

◆ Grade Level: 7–12, college
◆ Time Required for experiment: one class period to set up; months to observe

Answers to Questions

1. Most of the microbes were provided by the soil or, if you used it, by the commercial compost additive. The organisms that degrade vegetable matter are often bacteria in the genus *Bacillus* or are molds.

2. Meat scraps and bones will not interfere with the composting process. However, as they rot, they will smell very badly and may attract animals such as dogs and raccoons that will scatter the pile.

3. The microbes in the compost use the vegetable materials as a food source. They use the nitrogen in the proteins for growth and the carbohydrates as carbon and energy sources. Much of the carbon in the vegetable matter is converted to carbon dioxide gas and much of the nitrogen is converted to nitrate, which is the only form of nitrogen plants can use as a fertilizer.

4. Too much inorganic fertilizer can harm plants because it can cause an artificial imbalance of nutrients. The nutrients present in finished compost are much more balanced because they were produced by living organisms.

Key Terms

compost—a mixture of decomposing vegetation for fertilizing soil

fertilizer—any substance (manure, chemicals, or compost) used to enrich the soil

organic matter—any naturally occurring material containing carbon compounds

recycling—using a material more than one time

SOFT PRETZELS

◆ **Grade Level: 7–12**

◆ **Time Required for experiment: three hours**

This project is recommended because:

1. It fits easily into a morning or afternoon time frame. Total time is 2 to 3 hours, with several waiting periods that the class can use for ancillary activities.

2. Everyone can get involved in hand-twisting the dough prior to baking.

3. The yeasty aroma of the baking dough will perfuse the hallways of the institution, advertising to everyone the beneficial aspects of microbes.

 ## Precautions

The glaze for the pretzels should be prepared by the instructor (steps 9 and 10).

NOTE: Use gloves and goggles when preparing the sodium hydroxide solution. If material is spilled, clean up with water. If material is splashed on skin or in eyes, flush affected areas with large volumes of water and seek medical attention.

Procedure for Making Glaze

Mix 1 tablespoon sodium hydroxide (20 to 30 grams) into 1 liter cold tap water. The final concentration will be about 2 percent.

Comments for Instructor

You can save a great deal of time and avoid possible confusion, particularly when working with younger groups, if you prepare the dough ahead of time (steps 1 through 4 under **PROCEDURE** in the student pages).

A root beer project can be done by following the instructions on a bottle of root beer concentrate. Look in the spice section of your supermarket. The pizza project is interesting, and since the dough rises only once, it can be completed in the same time frame as the pretzels. But the pizza project does not include the twisting step and, therefore, will not involve as many individuals. The pizza toppings can be used to involve the entire class. However, the pizza project does not come out of the oven with the same "I made that one" sense of accomplishment provided by the pretzels project.

Answers to Questions

1. Other risen-dough products are breads and certain kinds of doughnuts. Yeast is also used in some kinds of crackers and in matzos, but the dough is not allowed to rise. Yeast is used in various beverages, including root beer, beers and ales, and wines. Yeast cells themselves are a good source of nutrients and are often included in pet foods and used as a vitamin supplement for humans.

2. Like all living cells, yeast cells require sources of energy, carbon, nitrogen, and several other elements. The sugar in the dough provides most of the carbon and energy; the milk provides the nitrogen.

3. Budding is asexual division in which the genetic material is distributed equally between the two daughter cells but the cytoplasm does not divide equally. The smaller cell appears to be "budding" off the larger cell.

Key Terms

budding—a form of asexual reproduction in which a daughter cell develops as a small outgrowth or protrusion of the parent cell

iris diaphragm—shutter-like apparatus below the stage of the microscope that is used to control the amount of light which passes onto a specimen

nutrients—growth-supporting substances

yeast—unicellular fungus belonging to the class Ascomycetes

The Microbiology Picnic

INTRODUCTION

When most people think of **microbes**, they think of "germs," which they view as undesirable. Actually, most microbes do not cause disease and many are beneficial to the environment and to human life. For as long as the human race has been on Earth, people have been using the activities of microbes to produce beneficial products. In the mid-1800's, Louis Pasteur finally explained the science which we now know as "microbiology." This science deals with all the many types of microorganisms, both desirable and undesirable. It is concerned with the way these microorganisms behave and how they interact with one another and with other living things.

The following exercises involve activities using microbes that function as "good germs." They illustrate some of the beneficial properties of **bacteria** and **yeast** such as **fermentation**. Everyone will bring to class a food that in some way involved a microorganism in its preparation. Most of the menu items suggested in the materials section do not actually contain living organisms, but microbes such as yeast or bacteria were used to obtain the final product. Yeast, for example, are used in the preparation of bread, and bacteria are used to make vinegar. However, other foods, such as yogurt, cheeses, and root beer, actually contain live microbes that are not harmful to humans.

Objective

1. Identify a variety of beneficial microbes that are associated with food production.
2. Understand that not all microbes are harmful.

Precautions

Many of the food items brought to the picnic will require **refrigeration** if they are to be stored longer than an hour before use. Many foods, if left at room temperature, can support growth of microbial populations, which can spoil food and possibly cause human illness. With the proper precautions and common sense, no threat to health will be involved with this project.

Microbes at the picnic

Materials (Work individually.)

1. Picnic supplies for eating: paper plates, knives, forks, spoons, napkins
2. Biohazard bag
3. Refrigeration capability for short-term storage
4. Menu suggestions:

Food	Microorganism involved
blue cheese	bacteria, mold
bread	yeast
cheddar cheese	bacteria
cocoa beans	yeast
cottage cheese	bacteria
olives	bacteria
pickles	bacteria, yeast
root beer	yeast
sauerkraut	bacteria
sausages	bacteria
sour cream	bacteria
soy sauce	molds, yeast, bacteria
swiss cheese	bacteria
vinegar	bacteria
yogurt	bacteria

Procedure

1. Decide what you would like to bring to the picnic to share with the class.

2. Learn how the microbe was used in preparation of the food. There are some references at the end of this project that may provide information.

3. Nobody will want to eat plain vinegar or soy sauce. Bring a food that uses substances like these in the recipe, such as salad dressings or marinades.

4. On the day of the picnic, bring your item to class along with anything that will be needed to serve it, such as a large spoon or a supply of paper cups.

5. Properly refrigerate all foods prior to the picnic. Leftovers should also be refrigerated.

Questions

1. Why does yeast cause bread dough to rise?

2. What is meant by "fermentation"? What is its significance in food preparation?

3. What may happen to some foods if they are not refrigerated?

4. What do some bacteria produce that causes foods such as pickles and vinegar to taste sour?

Key Terms

bacteria
fermentation
microbes
refrigeration
yeast

Suggested Readings

Alcamo, I. E. *Fundamentals of Microbiology.* 4th ed., Benjamin Cummings, Menlo Park, CA, 1994.

Gillen, A. L., and Williams, R. P. "Dinner Date with a Microbe." *The American Biology Teacher*, vol. 55, no. 5, 1993. Pages 268–274.

James, D. E. "Making Cheese in the Classroom." *Carolina Tips,* Vol. 48, no. 1, 1985.

Prescott, L. M., Harley, J. P., and Klein, D. A. *Microbiology.* 3rd ed., Wm. C. Brown, Dubuque, IA, 1996.

Walsh, P. M., and Hoover, D. G. "Bacterial Starter Cultures." Chapter 20, in *Food Biotechnology*, D. Knorr, ed. Marcel Dekker, New York, NY, 1987.

Composting

INTRODUCTION

Composting is an amazing natural process by which many kinds of bad-smelling things turn into sweet-smelling soil. The process starts with garbage and organic trash (like grass clippings) and ends with a crumbly substance that is sometimes called "black gold." When you use this natural product on gardens or potted plants, you don't need to worry about using too much of it, as you do with inorganic **fertilizers**. It also makes an attractive mulch.

Compost piles are collections of plant materials and solids that are allowed to decompose by the natural activities of beneficial microbes. Compost can be made in a bin such as a circle of chicken wire or snow fence or even an old garbage can. Practically any container of any size will do as long as it has plenty of holes in its sides to allow air to circulate. In this experiment, the compost container is made from a large plastic soda bottle.

Objective

1. Demonstrate the beneficial role of microorganisms in **recycling** waste materials into usable products.
2. Understand the process of decomposition.

Learning About Microbes

Materials (Work individually or in pairs.)

1. Two 1- or 2-liter plastic soda bottles—both must be the same size
2. Some **organic matter**—grass clippings, leaves, vegetable garbage
3. Scissors
4. Soil
5. Boiling water
6. Permanent marker

Procedure

1. Using scissors, remove the neck and opening of one of the soda bottles. Cut completely around the "shoulder" of the bottle, about an inch above the label (recycle the top part). Leave the thick, colored plastic bottom in place.
2. Remove the colored plastic bottom from the other bottle by heating the bottle in boiling water and then pulling the bottom off. The bottom you removed from the second bottle will be the lid for the cylinder you made from the first bottle.
3. Using sharp scissors, cut a number of slits or holes in the side of the cylinder.
4. Build the compost:
   (a) Place 1 inch of crunched leaves, grass clippings, or garbage into the bottom of the cylinder.
   (b) On top, place 1/2 inch of soil. At this point, it would be interesting to prepare a second cylinder to which a commercial compost starter is added. Alternatively, half the class could use the commercial starter and the other half could leave it out.
   (c) Repeat steps (a) and (b), creating layers, until the bottle is about 3/4 full. You can use anything for the organic layers, but avoid meat and bones. Use vegetable materials so there will not be a problem with flies, bad smells, or, if you were doing this on a large scale in your backyard, dogs and wild animals.
5. Add enough water to soak the whole pile.
6. Mark on the bottle where the top level of the pile is with a permanent marker.
7. Periodically add water to keep the compost damp and shake the bottle to keep air circulating through it.
8. After several weeks, examine the results.

Observations/Conclusions

1. Has the pile of organic matter expanded or compacted? Why?

2. What is the consistency of the composted material compared with the original materials put in several weeks ago?

3. All of this garbage and soil has been "rotting" for several weeks. Does it smell rotten? If so, why?

Questions

1. Of the materials layered in the bottle, which were sources of the microbes that were responsible for the decomposition of vegetable matter?

2. If you were making compost in your backyard, why is it a bad idea to include meat scraps and bones?

3. When leaves and other plant materials degrade, what happens to them? What happens to the proteins and carbohydrates?

Learning About Microbes

Chow's on

Happiness is a mulch pile!

4. Why is a large amount of finished compost safe to use as fertilizer, but a large amount of inorganic fertilizer (the kind you can buy at a garden store) possibly harmful to plants?

Key Terms

compost
fertilizer
organic matter
recycling

Suggested Readings

Arms, K. *Environmental Science*. Saunders, Philadelphia, PA, 1990.

Ingram, M. *Bottle Biology*. University of Wisconsin-Madison, Dept. of Plant Pathology, Madison, WI, 1993.

"The Magic of Composting." *Science and Children,* March 1987.

Soft Pretzels

A Classroom Project with Yeast

INTRODUCTION

Common bakers' **yeast**, or *Saccharomyces cerevisiae*, is one of the most readily available microorganisms and probably one that is most familiar to you. Yeast is used to brew root beer, make pizza dough, and bake soft pretzels.

Objectives

1. Demonstrate the beneficial activities of yeast.
2. Observe the effects of oxygen and warmth on rising dough.

Materials (makes 5 dozen pretzels)

For the dough:

1. 1½ sticks margarine, soft
2. 1⅓ cups of powdered milk
3. 1 quart hot tap water
4. ½ cup sugar
5. 12 cups of flour (about 5 pounds) divided into two 6-cup batches
6. 2 packages dry yeast
7. ½ tsp. baking powder
8. shortening (to grease baking sheets)

 For the glaze (prepared by the teacher):

1. sodium hydroxide, 20 to 30 grams
2. tap water

For sprinkling:

coarse salt

For mixing/baking:

Large bowl, greased baking sheets and oven or convection oven

For the yeast experiment:

1. freeze-dried yeast
2. warm water
3. Pasteur pipet
4. glass slide
5. cover slip
6. microscope

© 1998 J. Weston Walch, Publisher

Learning About Microbes

Procedure

1. Make sure the water is hot enough to melt the margarine. Mix the first four ingredients in a large bowl

2. Add 6 cups of the flour and the yeast. Mix well. Cover and let rise in a warm place for about 30 minutes.

3. Add the remaining flour and the baking powder. Mix thoroughly using both hands.

4. Cover the dough and let it rise again in a warm area until it is almost doubled in size (1½ to 2 hours).

5. Divide the dough into 6 equal pieces.

6. Divide each of the pieces into about 10 portions of equal size.

7. Using the palms of your hands, roll each portion into a rope about ½ inch in diameter and 18 inches long.

8. Twist the rope into a pretzel shape and tuck the ends under.

 PRECAUTION: For safety reasons, it is advisable that the instructor dip the pretzels.

9. Dip the pretzels, one at a time, into a warm solution of sodium hydroxide and water. The alkali acts as a browning agent and, at the concentration used, will not remain on the pretzels in dangerous amounts.

10. Remove pretzels from the glazing solution and place them on greased baking sheets.

11. Sprinkle the pretzels with coarse salt.

12. Bake the pretzels in a hot oven (400°F) for 15 minutes or until well browned.

COROLLARY ACTIVITY—BUDDING OF YEAST

While the dough is rising, prepare wet mount slides of the yeast cells.

Procedure

1. Add 1 or 2 grains of freeze-dried yeast to some warm water.

2. Wait until the mixture begins to become cloudy and bubbly. This may take ½ hour to 1 hour.

3. Using a Pasteur pipet, place a drop on a microscope slide and add a coverslip. With the **iris diaphragm** on your microscope nearly closed, a magnification of approximately 400X should be adequate to view the yeast cells. You should be able to see the cells reproducing asexually. This process is called **budding**.

Learning About Microbes

Observations/Conclusions

1. Did you notice any air bubbles in the risen dough? If so, what caused their formation?

2. Why was it necessary to knead the dough?

Questions

1. What other foods or beverages are made with yeast?

2. What ingredients in the dough are **nutrients** for the yeast?

3. What is "budding"?

Key Terms

budding
iris diaphragm
nutrients
yeast

Suggested Reading

Sunset Cook Book of Breads. Lane Magazine and Book Company, Menlo Park, CA, 1975.

Williams, R. P., and Gillen, A. L. "Microbe Phobia and Kitchen Microbiology." *The American Biology Teacher*, Vol. 53, no. 1, 1991, Pages 9–11.

Inhibition of Microbial Growth

INHIBITION OF MICROBIAL GROWTH

◆ Grade Level: 7–12, college
◆ Time Required for Experiment: one to three class periods, daily observation five to seven days

Included in this lab are three experiments to demonstrate the effects of different substances on microbial growth. The students in the class may be divided into groups so that all substances are tested simultaneously and the class can then compare the results of the different activities.

EXPERIMENT 1

Broth cultures of each organism may be prepared by inoculating tubes of Trypticase Soy broth with the appropriate culture and incubating overnight at 37°C.

Answers to Questions

1. The difference in the zone size observed for each bacterium is related to the relative antimicrobial activity of that antibiotic against that particular organism. Also, different antibiotics have varying degrees of antimicrobial activity against different species of organisms or even the same organism.

2. The physician may swab your throat and send the swab to a laboratory where the technician will carry out a test very similar to what you did in this experiment. The test would determine which antibiotic would be effective against the organism causing your sore throat.

3. Instructor: This is an open-ended question and, hopefully, will raise the student's consciousness about the many antibiotics available and the usefulness of these agents in treating infectious disease.

EXPERIMENT 2

Overnight broth cultures of the bacterial organisms may be prepared in the same manner as described in Experiment 1. The *Penicillium chrysogenum* culture should be grown on Sabouraud Dextrose agar for five to seven days.

Answers to Questions

1. Penicillin.

2. The material in the capsule is the same substance produced by the mold. The only difference is that the material in the capsule has been purified and standardized.

3. The differences are due to the relatively selective antimicrobial activity of the antibiotic against each organism.

4. The mold needed time to produce enough penicillin for an antimicrobial effect.

EXPERIMENT 3

A. Garlic

Materials

Broth cultures may be prepared by inoculating tubes of Trypticase Soy broth with the appropriate culture and incubating overnight at 37°C.

Answers to Questions

1. A natural antimicrobial substance produced by the garlic has an effect on the microorganism.
2. Instructor: Use this as a class discussion.

B. Chicken Soup

Have some students bring in homemade chicken soup and others bring in commercial varieties.

Materials

Broth cultures may be prepared by inoculating tubes of Trypticase Soy broth with the appropriate culture and incubating overnight at 37°C.

Answers to Questions

1. It is not known for certain, but the lipids (fats) in the soup may have an antimicrobial effect.

2. There have been reports in scientific literature about the beneficial effects of chicken soup on colds caused by viruses.

C. Lysozyme

Materials

1. Broth cultures may be prepared by inoculating tubes of Trypticase Soy broth with the appropriate culture and incubating overnight at 37°C.

2. Prepare two saline suspensions of *Micrococcus lysodeikitcus* and two suspensions of *Escherichia coli*. These may be prepared by aseptically transferring several drops of the overnight culture to the saline tubes using a sterile Pasteur pipet. (Enough should be added so that there is a visible cloudiness or turbidity.)

3. The egg white may be prepared by cracking the raw eggs carefully and separating the yolks from the whites using an egg separator. Aseptically prepare a 10 percent solution of egg white in sterile saline. Be sure there is sufficient egg white solution for the entire class.

Answers to Questions

1. It has an antimicrobial effect that protects the mucous membranes of the mouth (in saliva) and the eyes (in tears).

2. The strict definition of an antibiotic includes only substances produced by microorganisms. However, lysozyme definitely has antimicrobial activities that function in host defenses.

3. Unsaturated fatty acids in sebaceous secretions, lactic acid from sweat glands, lactoferrin in various body fluids, salivary peroxidase, etc.

Key Terms

agar—a dried extract of red algae used as the solidifying agent in various microbiological media

antibiotics—microbial products or their derivatives that kill susceptible microorganisms or inhibit their growth

antimicrobial—any chemical or physical agent that destroys microorganisms

culture—any growth or cultivation of organisms

gram-negative—bacteria that stain pink or red after performing the Gram stain. The bacterial cell walls are composed of a peptidoglycan layer surrounded by a lipopolysaccharide outer membrane. The differences in the cell wall composition of gram-positive and gram-negative bacteria determine their Gram reaction.

gram-positive—bacteria that stain purple after performing the Gram stain. The bacterial cell walls are composed of peptidoglycan and teichoic acids.

lysozyme—an enzyme with antimicrobial activities; found in egg whites, tears, and saliva

parasitism—an interactive relationship between two organisms or populations in which one is harmed and the other benefits

seeding—inoculation of bacteria on a petri dish in an even fashion covering the entire surface of the plate

sterile—free of living organisms

stock culture—a pure culture of a microorganism that has been stored at refrigerator temperature until ready for use

streaking—inoculation of the surface of a solid medium in such a way that individual colonies form on at least part of the surface during incubation

symbiosis—an interactive association between members of two populations producing a stable condition in which the two organisms live together in close proximity to their mutual advantage

synergism—a biological effect that occurs when two or more antibiotics acting together produce greater inhibitory effects on a given organism than the sum of the effects of the antibiotics; or an interactive but nonobligatory association between two populations in which each population benefits

zone of inhibition of growth—area of no bacterial growth around an antimicrobial agent

Inhibition of Microbial Growth

INTRODUCTION

Microorganisms, and even higher organisms, are affected by and affect other neighboring organisms. Some of these relationships, such as **symbiosis**, **parasitism**, and **synergism** may be familiar to you. Microbial populations of both plants and animals are determined by the mutual relationships of the organisms and their environments.

Some microorganisms produce substances that inhibit the growth of other microorganisms. These products, which we call **antibiotics**, are used in the treatment of infectious disease. The effectiveness of an **antimicrobial** substance can be determined by **streaking** bacteria onto a petri plate and then placing a disk that contains the antibiotic on the surface of the **agar.** After 24 hours of incubation at the proper temperature, the plate is examined for an area where the bacteria do not grow, called the **zone of inhibition of growth**. This is called the disk diffusion method of determining antimicrobial susceptibility.

A considerable number of plants and foods produce antimicrobial substances that inhibit the growth of bacteria. Foods such as chicken and garlic contain substances that are active in this respect. **Lysozyme** is an enzyme with antimicrobial activities. It breaks the bonds of bacterial cell walls and is found in egg whites, tears, and saliva.

The experiments in these exercises include a demonstration of the antimicrobial action of the material in an antibiotic capsule as well as naturally occurring antimicrobial substances produced by plants and humans to determine their inhibitory effects on the bacteria tested.

Precautions

1. Note the general safety precautions in the first chapter of this manual, especially in relation to use of Bunsen burners, use of safety glasses, and handwashing with appropriate antimicrobial soap solutions prior to and after lab.
2. Do not attempt any of the following experiments until you have learned proper aseptic technique.
3. Remember that even nonpathogenic bacteria can cause infections if not properly handled.

EXPERIMENT 1: ANTIBACTERIAL ACTIVITY OF A COMMERCIALLY AVAILABLE ANTIBIOTIC CAPSULE

Objectives

1. Demonstrate antimicrobial action of a familiar form of antibiotic, such as a capsule.
2. Inoculate a lawn of bacteria.
3. Observe the effects of an antibiotic on two different types of bacteria.
4. Recognize zones of inhibition of growth.
5. Use disks to evaluate differences in antimicrobial activity.

Materials (Students work individually or in pairs.)

1. Trypticase Soy Agar (TSA) plates [2]
2. Overnight cultures of *Escherichia coli* and/or *Staphylococcus epidermidis*

 3. Capsules of penicillin V-K or ampicillin (can be outdated material)*

4. Sterile paper disks (may be punched out from filter paper)
5. Sterile cotton swabs
6. Forceps
7. China marker
8. Biohazard bag
9. Distilled water
10. Sterile test tube
11. Bunsen burner
12. Masking tape
13. Ethyl alcohol in beakers

 *Penicillin-sensitive or immunocompromised individuals should not handle these materials!

Procedure

1. Label the bottom of one TSA plate with your name, the date, and *S. epidermidis*.
2. Using aseptic technique, dip a sterile cotton swab into the overnight culture of *S. epidermidis*. As you withdraw the swab from the tube, press the swab against the inside of the tube to squeeze out any excess fluid.

3. Open one of the petri dishes like a clam shell and completely streak the surface of the nutrient agar with the inoculated swab. See diagram below.

starting of a lawn of bacteria

4. Close the lid, rotate the plate, and streak again. Repeat this procedure at least two more times to ensure that the surface is completely covered and will grow as a lawn of bacteria. See diagrams below.

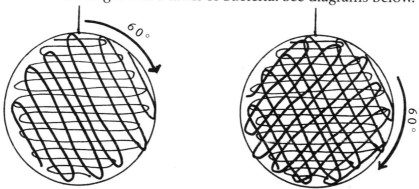

completing a lawn of bacteria

5. Label the bottom of another TSA plate with your name, the date, and *E. coli.*

6. Repeat steps 2 and 3 using the *E. coli* overnight culture.

7. Open a capsule of penicillin V-K or ampicillin and pour the contents into 10 ml of sterile distilled water in a test tube. As demonstrated by your instructor, flame-sterilize the forceps. (Forceps are dipped briefly into the ethyl alcohol, then touched to the flame and the alcohol allowed to burn off. This process is repeated twice.) Use the forceps to dip a blank paper disk into the antibiotic solution and to place the disk on the agar plate **seeded** with the **gram-positive** organism *(S. epidermidis).* Using the flame-sterilized forceps, gently tap the disk so it adheres to the agar. Reflame the forceps and repeat the procedure with another filter paper disk and place this disk on the plate seeded with the **gram-negative** organism *(E. coli).*

8. On each seeded plate, place a second filter disk that has been dipped into a tube of sterile distilled water only. This serves as a control disk.

9. Tape the plates closed using two small pieces of masking tape.

10. Incubate the plates in an upside-down position for 24 hours at 37°C.

Observations/Conclusions

1. Observe the effect of the disks on the growth of the bacteria on the plates.

2. If inhibition of growth occurred, record the diameter of the zone of inhibition, in millimeters, in Table 1 of the Laboratory Report Form.

3. Is there a difference between the zones around the antibiotic disk and the water disk? Why?

4. Are there any differences between the antibiotic disk zone sizes on the two different plates?

Questions

1. Why is there a difference between the sizes of the zones of inhibition of growth for the two bacteria?

2. What would be the value of this experiment if you had a sore throat?

3. Can you name an antibiotic that has been prescribed for you or a member of your family?

EXPERIMENT 2: PHENOMENON OF ANTIBIOSIS

Objectives

1. Observe the antagonistic effects of natural substances produced by microorganisms on the life processes of other organisms.
2. Recognize the differences between bacterial and fungal growth.

Materials (Work in pairs.)

1. Trypticase Soy Agar (TSA) plates [3]
2. Overnight cultures of *Escherichia coli*, *Staphylococcus epidermidis*, and *Micrococcus luteus*
3. **Stock culture** of the mold *Penicillium chrysogenum*
4. Inoculating loops
5. Bunsen burners
6. China markers
7. Biohazard bag
8. Masking tape

Procedure

1. Label the bottom of a TSA plate with your name, the date, and *P. chrysogenum*.
2. Flame-sterilize and cool an inoculating loop. Open the *P. chryso-genum* culture plate like a clam shell and scrape off some of the growth.
3. Open the TSA plate and streak the material in the loop in a straight line down the center of the plate.
4. Tape the plate together using two small pieces of masking tape.
5. Incubate the plate upside down at 25°C for 48 to 72 hours or until growth of the mold first appears.

6. On the bottom of the plate, draw three evenly spaced lines perpendicular to the mold growth and label the lines with the names of the three different bacterial cultures.

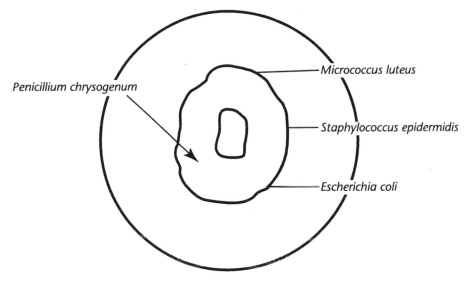

Penicillium chrysogenum

Micrococcus luteus

Staphylococcus epidermidis

Escherichia coli

7. Using aseptic technique, streak a small amount of *E. coli* on the surface of the agar directly over the line on the bottom of the petri dish. Start the inoculation at the edge of the mold culture and streak the bacteria to the edge of the petri dish.

8. Repeat step 7 for *S. epidermidis* and *M. luteus*.

9. Tape the plates closed using two small pieces of masking tape and incubate the plates upside down for 24 to 48 hours at 37°C or in a warm place.

Observations/Conclusions

1. Observe any difference in the growth patterns of the three different types of bacteria in relation to how close each grew to the edge of the mold culture.

2. Record the lines of growth observed on the TSA plate using Table 2 of the Laboratory Report Form.

3. When you go home, open your refrigerator and see whether you can find a piece of moldy fruit or cheese. Does the mold growth look similar to that on the petri dish?

Learning About Microbes

Questions

1. What antimicrobial substance is the mold producing? Research this substance in your library, then discuss some of its history.

2. What is the relationship between the substance produced by the mold and the material in the capsule you used in Experiment 1?

   What is the source of the capsule and the material in it?

3. If there are differences in growth patterns, how do you explain them?

4. Why did the mold *P. chrysogenum* have to be streaked down the center of the agar plate 2 days prior to cross-streaking with the bacteria?

EXPERIMENT 3: ANTIMICROBIAL ACTION OF SUBSTANCES PRODUCED BY PLANT, ANIMAL, AND MAN

Objectives

1. Demonstrate that natural substances produced by plants, animals, and humans may also possess antimicrobial substances.
2. Use disks to evaluate differences in antimicrobial activity.
3. Recognize zones of inhibition of growth.

A. Garlic

Materials (Work in pairs.)

1. Trypticase Soy Agar (TSA) plates [2]
2. Overnight cultures of *Escherichia coli* and *Micrococcus luteus*
3. Sterile cotton swabs
4. Bunsen burner
5. Cloves of garlic
6. China marker
7. Knife
8. Forceps
9. Biohazard bag
10. Masking tape
11. Beakers of ethyl alcohol

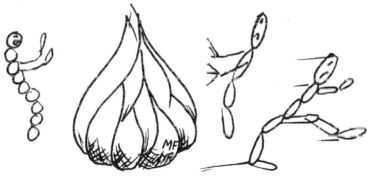

Procedure

1. Label the bottom of one TSA plate with your name, the date, and *M. luteus*.
2. Using aseptic technique, dip a sterile cotton swab into the overnight culture of *M. luteus*. As you withdraw the swab from the tube, press it against the inside of the tube to squeeze out excess fluid.

Learning About Microbes

3. Create a lawn on the TSA plate using the technique previously demonstrated by the instructor. Discard the swab in the biohazard bag.

4. Label a second TSA plate with your name, the date, and *E. coli.*

5. Repeat steps 2 and 3 using the stock culture of *E. coli.*

6. Cut a garlic clove in two, crosswise; then cut off a second section about 1/8 inch thick. Using flame-sterilized forceps, gently press this section onto the surface of the agar plate that was inoculated with *M. luteus.* Discard this piece of garlic in the biohazard bag.

7. Cut another section of garlic and place it on the surface of the plate inoculated with *E. coli,* then discard this piece in the biohazard bag.

8. Tape the two plates together using two small pieces of masking tape and incubate in an upside-down position at 35°C for 24 to 48 hours.

Observations/Conclusions

1. After incubation, examine the plates and record the results in Table 3 of the Laboratory Report Form.

2. Place the plates back in the incubator at 25°C and examine again after 5 to 7 days. Record these results in Table 3 as well.

Questions

1. What is causing the zone of inhibition of growth produced by the garlic?

2. Ask your parents, grandparents, or friends if they use garlic for any of its beneficial effects.

B. Chicken Soup

Materials (Work in pairs.)

1. Trypticase Soy Agar (TSA) plates [2]
2. Overnight cultures of *Escherichia coli* and *Micrococcus luteus*
3. Sterile filter paper disks
4. Sterile cotton swabs
5. Tube of sterile water
6. Forceps
7. Masking tape
8. Bunsen burner
9. Chicken soup samples (commercial and homemade)
10. China marker
11. Biohazard bag
12. Beakers of ethyl alcohol

Procedure

1. Draw lines on the bottom of a TSA plate to divide it into three sections. Label the sections "Soup #1," "Soup #2," and "water control." Also label the bottom of the plate with your name, the date, and *M. luteus*.

2. Using aseptic technique, dip a sterile cotton swab into the overnight culture of *M. luteus*. As you withdraw the swab from the tube, press it against the inside of the tube to squeeze out excess fluid.

3. Create a lawn on the TSA plate using the technique previously demonstrated by the instructor.

4. Repeat steps 1 to 3 using *E. coli*.

5. Using flame-sterilized forceps, moisten a disk by dipping it into soup sample #1 (commercial) to soak up some fluid. Place the disk on the inoculated plate of *M. luteus* in the appropriate section. Using the forceps, tap down the disk so it adheres to the agar surface.

6. Reflame the forceps each time and, using two new disks, repeat step 5 for soup sample #2 (homemade) and the water control.

7. Repeat steps 5 to 6 for the *E. coli* plate.

8. Tape the two plates together using two small pieces of masking tape and incubate in an upside-down position at 35°C for 24 to 48 hours.

Learning About Microbes

Observations/Conclusions

1. Look for zones of inhibition of growth around each paper disk and measure the diameter of the zone in millimeters

2. Record results in Table 4 of the Laboratory Report Form.

Questions

1. If the chicken soup produced a zone of inhibition of growth, what do you think is in the soup that is responsible for this effect?

2. If you had a cold, do you think eating chicken would help cure you?

C. Lysozymes

Materials (Work in pairs.)

1. Saline suspensions of overnight cultures of *Escherichia coli* and *Micrococcus lysodeikitcus* (2 of each)

2. Tube of sterile saline (0.85% NaCl)

3. Pasteur pipets (4)

4. 10% solution of egg whites*

5. China marker

6. Biohazard bag

*Tears would be equally effective and may be substituted for the egg whites; however, it may be more difficult to collect sufficient material.

Don't cry over me

Procedure

1. Label one saline suspension of *M. lysodeikitcus* with your name and "Egg."
2. Using a sterile Pasteur pipet, add 4 to 5 drops of the 10% solution of egg whites to the tube.
3. Label one saline suspension of *M. lysodeikitcus* with your name and "Control."
4. Using a new, sterile Pasteur pipet, add 4 to 5 drops of sterile saline to the tube.
5. Repeat steps 1 to 4 using the saline suspension of *E. coli*.
6. Gently agitate the four tubes and examine at 10-minute intervals for the next 30 minutes, comparing the cloudiness (turbidity) of the control suspension with the corresponding test suspension.

Observations/Conclusions

1. Record results in Table 5 of the Laboratory Report Form.
2. Did you note any clearing or decrease in turbidity in either of the bacterial suspensions? If so, how do you account for this?

Questions

1. Can you suggest a beneficial use for the lysozyme contained in saliva or tears?

2. Would lysozyme be considered a "true" antibiotic? Why or why not?

3. Research medical microbiology texts for mention of other natural substances in or on the human body that function as host defense agents.

Key Terms

agar
antibiotics
antimicrobial
culture
gram-negative
gram-positive
lysozyme
parasitism
seeding
sterile
stock culture
streaking
symbiosis
synergism
zone of inhibition of growth

Suggested Readings

Abraham, E. P. "The Beta-Lactam Antibiotics." *Scientific American*, June 1981, pp 76–86.

Brooks, G. F., Butal, J., and Ornston, L. O. *Jawetz, Melnick and Adelberg's Medical Microbiology.* 19th ed., Appleton, Lang and Co., Norwalk, CT, 1991, pp 149–180.

Microbiology Laboratory Report Form

Name _____ Date _____

Experiment 1

TABLE 1		
ORGANISM	ANTIBIOTIC ZONE SIZE	WATER ZONE SIZE
Escherichia coli		
Staphylococcus epidermidis		

Experiment 2

TABLE 2	
ORGANISM	DRAWING OF BACTERIAL AND MOLD GROWTH
Escherichia coli	
Micrococcus luteus	
Staphylococcus epidermidis	

Experiment 3A: Garlic

TABLE 3		
ORGANISM	ZONE SIZE—48 HRS	ZONE SIZE—7 DAYS
Micrococcus luteus		
Escherichia coli		

Experiment 3B: Soup

TABLE 4			
ORGANISM	SOUP #1 ZONE SIZE	SOUP #2 ZONE SIZE	WATER CONTROL ZONE SIZE
Escherichia coli			
Micrococcus luteus			

Experiment 3C: Lysozyme

TABLE 5				
Use the following key to describe the amount of turbidity: most turbidity = +++ moderate turbidity = ++ slight turbidity = + no turbidity = −				
ORGANISM	TEARS	TEARS CONTROL	EGG WHITE	EGG WHITE CONTROL
Escherichia coli				
Micrococcus lysodeikitcus				

Learning About Microbes

Microbes in the Environment

MICROBES IN THE ENVIRONMENT: THE DISTRIBUTION OF MICROORGANISMS IN THE ENVIRONMENT

◆ **Grade Level:** 7–12, college

◆ **Time Required for Experiment:** minimum of two lab periods

The first period requires about 45 minutes and is devoted to student sampling of various environments for the presence of microbes and then inoculating culture media with their samples. Students may also expose media to the air in different areas to determine if microbes are present there. The second period requires 45 to 60 minutes and focuses on an evaluation of the results. To effectively emphasize the major theme of this exercise, students must observe microbial growth not only in their own cultures, but also in those of their classmates.

Divide the class into four groups: A, B, C, and D.

If a 37°C incubator is not available, the nutrient broth and TSA or Nutrient agar cultures can be incubated at room temperature. Streptococci from the throat will generally grow poorly at room temperature. After proper incubation, all cultures should exhibit growth.

Answers to Questions

1. Microbes are indeed ubiquitous. Everywhere we looked, we found them to be present since all cultures exhibited evidence of growth. We did achieve the objectives of this experiment.

2. The agar gives a better assessment of growth because of the specific colonial characteristics exhibited by the various microbes isolated. In turbid broth, one has no idea how many different microorganisms may be growing in the tube.

3. Microbes will adhere more readily to a wet surface than a dry one.

4. The plates with the greatest number of colonies are usually those that have been in contact with the skin, (lips, nose, fingers, etc.). On these plates, many colonies overlap, all growing on the surface area of the agar that was in direct contact with the body. Look for the individual colonies. The external human body, with its sweat glands, oil, and waste secretions plus other nutrients, provides an excellent habitat for microbial growth. Dust generally yields many large fungal (mold) colonies which are single colonies, and much larger than most bacterial colonies.

5. Plates exposed to various air samples may have no growth due to the lack of air currents at the time the sample was taken. Also, samples from frequently washed hands quite frequently will have little turbidity in broth. This is where comparison with a sterile broth tube is helpful.

6. 37°C (98.6°F) is human body temperature. Microbes in contact with the human body grow best at this temperature.

7. A petri dish provides a closed chamber for microbial growth. It allows gases from the air to enter but not contaminating airborne microbes. It can be used to grow pure cultures (only one microbial species at a time) or mixed cultures.

8. Fungal colonies generally have a dry, cottony appearance due to the hyphae (filamentous, cellular, thread-like structures) they produce. They can exhibit a variety of pigments, depending on the type of mold. Bacterial colonies are generally smaller, and have a smoother, more shiny appearance. They are nonfilamentous. They also can exhibit a variety of different pigments, depending on the species.

9. The agar medium used for microbial growth is dissolved in water when prepared. At the warmer incubation temperatures, the water condenses out of solution and the moisture tends to accumulate on the lid of the agar plates. If this moisture drips onto the agar surface where the colonies are growing, it will cause the colonies to mix together producing a solution resembling turbid broth on the agar surface. Incubating the plates upside down prevents this water from touching the agar surface where the colonies are growing.

NOTE: You may wish to have students submit their observations/conclusions on a separate sheet of paper.

Key Terms

agar—dried extract of red algae used as the solidifying agent in various microbiological media

anthrax—infectious disease of animals, such as cattle and sheep, caused by *Bacillus anthracis* and transmissible to man by the handling of infected products

aseptic technique—method to keep out unwanted microorganisms

Bacillus anthracis—a gram-positive, spore-forming, aerobic bacillus

bacteria (*pl.* of **bacterium**)—unicellular organisms, belonging to kingdom *Monera*, that have no organized nucleus (procaryotic cells)

blood agar—an enriched medium, composed of Trypticase Soy agar plus 5 percent sheep red blood cells; for the growth of fastidious bacteria or for distinguishing various types of hemolysis

colonial morphology—form and structure of a colony of bacteria or fungi

colony—visible mass of cells that comes from the increased number of cells after cell division

contaminate—to introduce undesirable microbes into a controlled environment

culture—any growth or cultivation of organisms

culture media—growth media for the cultivation of microorganisms

ecological niche—the habitat or role of an organism within its particular community

enzyme—a protein that catalyzes a chemical reaction in a living organism

fastidious—having very specific or demanding requirements for growth

fomite—a nonliving object capable of acting in the spread of disease

fungus (*pl.* is **fungi**)—any of the saprophytic or parasitic members belonging to kingdom *Fungi* that lack chlorophyll and have a nuclear membrane; includes molds, rusts, mildew, smuts, mushrooms, and yeast

Germ theory—the theory that microorganisms cause disease

in vitro—literally "in glass." Outside of a living body and in an artificial environment.

inoculate—to introduce microorganisms into a culture medium or host

macroscopic—visible with the naked eye

microbe or microorganism—any of the bacteria, protozoa, viruses, or various fungi and algae

nutrient agar and broth—a general, all-purpose culture medium composed of beef extract and peptone, in solid or liquid form, and able to support the growth of many types of bacteria

sterile—free of living organisms

streptococci—a family of gram-positive cocci whose cells occur as pairs or chains, exhibiting facultative anaerobic, fermentative metabolism

Streptococcus—the genus name of the gram-positive cocci collectively referred to as streptococci

Trypticase Soy agar—a soybean-casein digest solid medium that supports the growth of various bacteria

ubiquitous—widespread

virulent pathogen—a microorganism capable of causing a disease marked by a rapid and severe course

The Distribution of Microorganisms in the Environment: How to Prove That Microorganisms are Ubiquitous

"I hear and I forget.
I see and I remember.
I do and I understand."

—ancient Chinese proverb

INTRODUCTION

Just about everywhere we could look on this planet, we would find **microorganisms** such as **bacteria** and **fungi** (molds). They are everywhere, yet we can't see them. They are present in the air we breathe, on the lips we kiss, on the earth we walk on, in the food we eat, and even on the outside and inside of our own bodies. You are limited only by your own imagination as to where to look for **microbes**. You will see that they occupy **ecological niches** on all forms of life and in most environments. You can design your own experiments to discover the number and diversity of microbes all around us.

Being thoroughly aware of the distribution of microbes in our environment is important so that when we want to isolate, or grow *in vitro*, one single type of microbe such as the disease producer *Bacillus anthracis*, we will not **contaminate** our **cultures** with microbes from the environment.

In this exercise, microbes will be grown *in vitro* using both **agar** and broth **culture media**. After a suitable incubation period, broth will become turbid (cloudy) due to microbial growth, while on the solid media, **colonies** will be visible. Colonies are visible with the naked eye and each microbial species exhibits a particular **colonial morphology,** specific characteristics such as size, shape, and color. This difference in colonial characteristics helps us identify specific microbes.

The study of infectious disease and the microbes that caused them began in the nineteenth century. Louis Pasteur, a French scientist, proved that disease could arise from infection with microorganisms. In Europe, a deadly blood disease called **anthrax** was spreading through herds of cattle and sheep. Robert Koch, a German country doctor, was asked to find out what was causing this disease. Koch studied a large number of diseased animals and found a microscopic rod-shaped bacterium in the blood of each of them. This same organism was not found in any healthy animals. To study this organism and prove that it was the cause of the animals' disease, Koch had to grow it in his laboratory. This presented a challenge since no one before had tried to grow bacteria under controlled conditions. Microbes need nutrients for their growth, just like all living things. Koch originally used a combination of beef broth and gelatin which he thought would provide a solid surface for bacterial growth. Much to his dismay, he found that certain types of bacteria, such as the anthrax organism, produce a chemical substance that digests and liquefies gelatin. Gelatin also liquefies at the high temperatures required for the growth of many bacteria. One of Koch's associates, Walther Hesse, discussed this problem with his wife. She was fond of making jams and jellies using a Dutch recipe passed along to her by her mother. To "set" or solidify her jams, she used a seaweed-derived product called agar. So Koch tried using agar to form a solid medium for growing bacteria and found it worked! Once jelled, the medium stayed solid even at high temperatures. This combination of nutrients and agar is referred to as a culture medium.

Another associate, Robert Julius Petri, invented the culture plate (now called a petri dish) that was used to grow the bacteria Koch had isolated from the infected animals. The petri dish is still used today in labs all over the world as a chamber for growing microbes and preventing contamination of the culture with organisms from the environment.

To prove that the bacteria he cultured in the lab from the blood of the diseased animals was the cause of anthrax, Koch **inoculated** the lab-grown bacteria into healthy mice. Within a few hours the mice developed the symptoms of anthrax and died. These procedures, developed by Koch and his associates, are the basis of the **germ theory of infection**, proof that a specific microbe is the cause of a specific infectious disease.

Objectives

1. Prove that microbes are **ubiquitous** by testing air, various **fomites**, skin, and your nasopharynx for the presence of microorganisms.
2. Demonstrate the diversity of the microbial world by observing the cultural characteristics of various microbes isolated from these environments.

Precautions

1. Wear a disposable apron.
2. Wash your hands every time you enter or leave the lab with an antimicrobial soap such as liquid Dial®.
3. Wipe table tops thoroughly with Lysol®.
4. Do not leave lids of petri dishes open longer than necessary. (Do NOT put lids on the table.)
5. Dispose of used swabs immediately in appropriate containers. (Do NOT place swabs on the table.)
6. Autoclave all materials as soon as you no longer need them.

Materials (Work individually within your group.)

Group A Students:

1. **Sterile** petri dish (plate) containing **Nutrient agar** (NA) or **Trypticase Soy agar** (TSA)
2. China marker
3. 37°C incubator*

4. Biohazard bag
5. Masking tape

Group B Students:

1. Sterile petri dish (plate) containing Nutrient agar (NA) or Trypticase Soy agar (TSA)
2. Tube of sterile water
3. Sterile cotton swab

4. China marker
5. 37°C incubator*
6. Biohazard bag
7. Masking tape

---

*optional item

Group C Students:

1. Sterile Nutrient broth tubes
2. Sterile cotton swab
3. China marker
4. 37°C incubator*
5. Biohazard bag
6. Tube of sterile water
7. Test-tube rack

Group D Students:

1. Sterile **Blood agar** plates**
2. Sterile cotton swab
3. Tube of sterile water
4. China marker
5. Biohazard bag
6. 37°C incubator*
7. Test-tube rack

Procedure

Group A Students:

1. Label the bottom of the plate clearly with the name of the sample you will be testing, your name, and the date.
2. Now you will expose the sterile NA or TSA plate. Your instructor will direct you to do one of the following:
   (a) Open the plate to the air in the laboratory for 30 minutes.
   (b) Open the plate to the air in various rooms outside of the lab for 30 minutes (restrooms, library, cafeteria, etc.).
   (c) Open the plate to the air outside of the building for 30 minutes.
   (d) Place your fingertips or toes lightly against the agar surface.
   (e) Place 5 to 6 coins on the agar surface then replace the lid. Remove the coins after 30 minutes.
   (f) Comb or brush your hair for 15 seconds over the exposed agar plate.
   (g) Blow some dust on the exposed agar plate.
3. After completing the assignment, tape the lid of the plate to the base using 2 small pieces of masking tape.

Group B Students:

1. Label the bottom of the plate clearly with the name of the sample you will be testing, your name, and the date.
2. Moisten a sterile swab in the tube of sterile water and express most of the water out of it by pressing the swab against the inside wall of the tube.

---

*optional item
**TSA plates may be used

Learning About Microbes

3. Swab one of these surfaces:

sink	lab bench or table
water fountain	*outer surface* of nose
telephone grip	*outer surface* of ears
piece of jewelry	inside of your shoes
wristwatch	inside creases of elbows
telephone mouthpiece	inside creases of knees

4. Open the petri plate like a clam shell and using zigzag strokes, lightly rub the entire surface with the swab. Be careful not to break through the agar.

5. Discard the swab in a biohazard bag.

6. Tape the plate closed with 2 small pieces of masking tape.

Group C Students:

1. Label a tube of sterile nutrient broth clearly with the name of the sample you will be testing, your name, and the date.

2. Moisten the swab in the tube of sterile water and sample any surface from the Group B list.

3. Inoculate the tube of sterile Nutrient broth with the swab.

4. Keep the swab in the broth and replace the cap. If necessary, break off the stick end of the swab so that it will fit into the tube.

Group D Students:

Note on Blood agar: This medium contains a protein digest as a nutrient source, agar for solidification, and sheep red blood cells as an extra nutrient. It is considered a "gourmet" diet for the more **fastidious** (requiring special nutrients) bacteria such as ***Streptococcus***. Some species of **streptococci** live in the throat of most normal healthy individuals; other species are **virulent pathogens** that generally cause infection whenever they enter the body.

1. Label the bottom of the Blood agar plate clearly with the name of the sample you will be testing, your name, and the date.

2. Half of the students in your group should open the Blood agar plate, hold it approximately 6 inches from their mouth, and cough onto the agar surface 10 to 15 times.

3. Students from the other half of the group should moisten a sterile swab in sterile water and sample any surface from the Group B list. These students should then open the plate like a clam shell, lightly rub the surface of the agar with the swab, and dispose of the swab in the biohazard bag.

4. Tape each plate closed with two small pieces of masking tape.

For All Procedures: Invert all plates prior to incubation. All plates and tubes should be incubated for 48 hours at room temperature or in a 37°C incubator, if available. Your instructor should include uninoculated tubes and plates as controls.

Observations/Conclusions

After incubation, evaluate your cultures. Be sure to observe your own cultures plus those of other groups.

A. Groups "A" and "B"

1. Note the morphology of the colonies on the plates: size and shape, pigment, margin, configuration, etc. Refer to the illustration of colony characteristics found in the **Aseptic Technique** lab.
2. Are the colonies all the same size and color?
3. Can you differentiate between fungal and bacterial colonies?
4. What are some distinct characteristics of fungi that make them easily identifiable?
5. Determine the approximate number of each type of colony on your plate. Refer to the illustration of colony characteristics found in the Aseptic Technique lab. Fill in Table 1 of the Laboratory Report Form.

B. Group "C"

1. Examine the tube of Nutrient broth. Is it clear or cloudy?
2. Compare it with a tube of sterile Nutrient broth. What is the significance of a cloudy tube of broth?
3. Fill in Table 2 of the Laboratory Report Form.

C. Group "D"

1. Note the morphology of the colonies on the plates: size and shape, pigment, margin, configuration, etc. Refer to the illustration of colony characteristics found in the Aseptic Technique lab.
2. Are the colonies all the same size and color?
3. Can you differentiate between fungal and bacterial colonies?
4. What are some distinct characteristics of fungi that make them easily identifiable?
5. Determine the approximate number of each type of colony on your plate. Refer to the illustration of colony characteristics found in the Aseptic Technique lab.
6. Fill in Table 3 of the Laboratory Report Form.

7. Look for the tiny, translucent colonies characteristic of streptococci. Also look at the color of the blood agar around the *Streptococcus* colonies. Is it still bright red? Many *Streptococcus* species have **enzymes** that break down and destroy red blood cells, creating either a clear or a green halo around the colony.

Questions

1. What conclusions can you draw after completing this exercise? Did you achieve the objectives of this experiment?

2. Which type of culture media—the broth or the agar—gives you a better assessment of the variety of different microorganisms present in an environment? Why?

3. Why were you told to first moisten the swabs with water before swabbing the samples tested?

4. Using the quantitative data recorded as your indicator, which sample had the greatest number of colonies? Why do you think this sample had such a high microbial count?

5. Did any of the cultures have no microbial growth? If so, can you speculate as to why no microbes were detected at this site?

6. Why is 37°C a desirable incubation temperature for the cultures?

7. What is the value of using petri plates in microbiology?

8. Describe some differences in the **macroscopic** appearance of bacterial and fungal colonies.

9. Why are inoculated petri plates incubated in an inverted position (agar side up)?

Learning About Microbes

Key Terms

agar

anthrax

aseptic technique

Bacillus anthracis

bacteria (bacterium)

Blood agar

colonial morphology

colony

contaminate

culture

culture media

ecological niche

enzyme

fastidious

fomite

fungus (fungi)

germ theory

in vitro

inoculate

macroscopic

microbe or microorganism

Nutrient agar and broth

sterile

streptococci

Streptococcus

Trypticase Soy agar

ubiquitous

virulent pathogen

THE FAR SIDE By GARY LARSON

THE FAR SIDE © (1986) FARWORKS, INC. Used by permission. All rights reserved

"You call this a niche?"

Suggested Readings

Benson, H. *Microbiological Applications*. 7th ed., William C. Brown, Dubuque, IA, 1998.

Johnson, T., and Case, C. *Laboratory Experiments in Microbiology*. 5th ed., Benjamin Cummings, Menlo Park, CA, 1998.

Tortora, G. J., Funke, B. R., and Case, C. L. *Microbiology*. 6th ed., Benjamin Cummings, Menlo Park, CA, 1997.

Microbiology Laboratory Report Form

Name _____ Date _____

TABLE 1—NA or TSA Plate

Record your count of colonies using the following scale:

0 = no growth	+++ = 51–100 colonies
+ = 1–10 colonies	TNTC (Too numerous to count) = more than 100 colonies
++ = 11–50 colonies	

	BACTERIAL COLONY	FUNGAL COLONY
Count		
Size		
Color		
Appearance		

◆ 83 ◆ *Learning About Microbes*

TABLE 2—Nutrient Broth

Observe your broth for evidence of microbial growth. Record your results plus those of other students in your group using the following code:

+ = growth (turbid broth)   **– = no growth (clear broth)**

SAMPLE	RESULTS	SAMPLE	RESULTS

TABLE 3—Blood Agar

Observe types of colonies on your plate. Record below using the same quantitative scale used for Table 1.

COLONY	COUGH	ENVIRONMENTAL SAMPLE
Count		
Size		
Color		
Appearance		

Transmission and Control of Microbes

TRANSMISSION AND CONTROL OF MICROBES: INTERRUPTION OF THE TRANSMISSION OF MICROORGANISMS

◆ **Grade Level: 10–12, college**
◆ **Time Required for Experiment: one hour for setup; two days for incubation; one hour for reading and interpretation**

Precautions

1. Bleach may be irritating to the skin and eyes. Avoid contact with skin, face, and clothing. First aid: If splashed in eye, flush with water for 15 minutes. If ingested, drink glass of water and call physician. Do not mix with other chemicals since hazardous gases may result.

2. Have students place all bacterial cultures and associated contaminated materials in a bio-hazard bag. If you do not have an autoclave, dispose of contaminated materials by bringing them to the closest laboratory, e.g., a private medical testing laboratory, a college or university laboratory, or a hospital clinical laboratory for decontamination and/or proper disposal of such waste. If you are distant from any of the above, a physician's office may be able to help you dispose of these materials. Pending disposal, materials should be stored at 4°C away from foods and drinks.

Note: Divide class into four groups: **A, B, C,** and **D.**

EXPERIMENT 1

Procedure

Assign several students to check for bacterial growth on a daily basis. See flow chart below.

Answers to Questions

1. Bacterial cells grow on agar containing a variety of nutrients including sources of carbon, vitamins, and growth factors. These cells may be recognized by their appearance as round, raised elevations on top of the agar surface. Other characteristics may vary (e.g., degree of opacity, color, and moistness).

2. No. The colonies look dissimilar because many different types of bacteria live in the same medium or environment (e.g. in food or water or on the surface of human bodies). The colony of each bacterial type may have a different appearance (e.g., size, shape, and color).

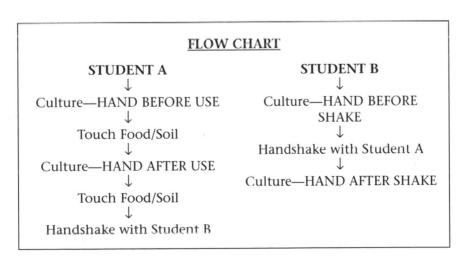

FLOW CHART

STUDENT A	STUDENT B
↓	↓
Culture—HAND BEFORE USE	Culture—HAND BEFORE SHAKE
↓	↓
Touch Food/Soil	Handshake with Student A
↓	↓
Culture—HAND AFTER USE	Culture—HAND AFTER SHAKE
↓	
Touch Food/Soil	
↓	
Handshake with Student B	

3. The "after" cultures provide the highest number of organisms.

4. Yes. Direct contact (the handshake) with student A spreads microbes from the food or soil to student B.

5. The bacterial counts from the hands of students would have increased after they had shaken hands with student A, who touched food or soil.

EXPERIMENT 2

Procedure

Students should exchange data with other students to answer the questions. See flow chart below.

Answers to Questions

1. The "after use" cultures should have the greatest number of bacteria. The "before use" cultures should have the next highest number of bacteria. The "after wash" count will be the lowest.

2. Soap physically removes bacteria from hands. Antibacterial soaps further disinfectant and leave a protective film that effectively reduces the number of microbes for a period of time after handwashing. Consequently, handwashing does interfere with transmission of microbes between persons.

3. The bacterial counts of the hands of students X and A would increase after they

touched the used cutting board, but before washing.

4. Disinfectants physically remove and reduce the number of microbes. Disinfection of the cutting board interfered with the transmission of microbes from the board to persons touching the board.

Key Terms

antiseptic—disinfectant that can be applied to body surfaces

cholera—an acute, infectious gastrointestinal disease caused by the bacteria *Vibrio cholerae*, which is usually spread through contaminated water

contaminated material—material or medium that has been in contact with and is likely to contain infectious microbes

disinfectant—a chemical, often toxic, used on inanimate objects to kill vegetative forms of disease-producing microorganisms

disinfection—process of applying disinfectant to the environment to destroy disease-producing microorganisms

epidemic—large number of new cases of a communicable disease occurring for a brief period of time in a specific geographical area. Epidemics sometimes occur in a population only in the presence of certain conditions and infectious microbes. In contrast, endemic diseases are constantly present in small numbers of persons of a population.

Hycheck®—a contact agar paddle with a grid that permits a semi-quantitative estimate of

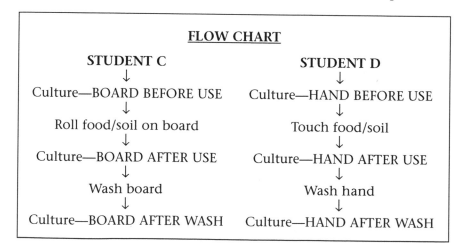

FLOW CHART

STUDENT C	STUDENT D
↓	↓
Culture—BOARD BEFORE USE	Culture—HAND BEFORE USE
↓	↓
Roll food/soil on board	Touch food/soil
↓	↓
Culture—BOARD AFTER USE	Culture—HAND AFTER USE
↓	↓
Wash board	Wash hand
↓	↓
Culture—BOARD AFTER WASH	Culture—HAND AFTER WASH

the number of bacterial cells present on environmental surfaces or in liquids; an alternative to RODAC® plates.

mucosal surface—a membrane rich in mucus glands that lines human or animal body passages and cavities that communicate directly or indirectly with the exterior (e.g., mucosa of the respiratory, gastrointestinal, and urogenital systems)

RODAC® plate—Replicate Organism Detection And Counting plate; contains a grid to permit precise location and counting of bacterial cells present on environmental surfaces

sewage contamination—direct contact of or mixture of sewage with water supply

source of contamination—original reservoir of infectious organisms that may lead to acquisition of infection by exposed person

vehicle—carrier of infectious organisms to humans

Interruption of the Transmission of Microorganisms

INTRODUCTION

During an 1885 London **epidemic** British physician John Snow proved that drinking water is a **vehicle** for the spread of **cholera**. In the first two months of the epidemic, more than 350 people died from cholera. Snow suspected that the excrement from cholera patients was highly infectious and that **sewage contamination** of the water supply might exist. In those days, raw sewage was dumped directly into London's Thames River. Most of the deaths occurred in houses supplied by two water companies. These two companies obtained their water from a section of the river in the heart of London, a heavily populated area. The third major company, supplying a large number of houses that had very few associated deaths, was found to obtain water from a point distant from the heart of the city. Consequently, water from the heart of London was thought to be the **source of contamination** and the cause of the epidemic. The epidemic was controlled by stopping the usage of water from the two questionable water companies. Sewage treatment procedures were eventually developed to prevent the occurrence of future waterborne epidemics.

Microorganisms are present on the entire surface of the human body and its **mucosal surfaces**. In addition, microbes are present in the environment—in our food and water, in the soil, and in and on the surfaces of animals and plants. Spread of microorganisms between people may occur through close contact (e.g., coughing, sneezing, and handshaking). Spread from the environment to man may occur through touching of **contaminated materials**, ingestion of contaminated food or drink, or inhalation of contaminated air.

Petri dishes or tubes containing Nutrient agar are used to grow microorganisms (e.g. bacteria, yeast, and molds). This experiment will be restricted to testing for the presence of bacteria. Agar plates will be partially filled with sterile Nutrient agar and the material to be cultured will be placed on the agar and spread across its surface. If the petri dish is filled so that the surface of the growth medium is raised over the edge of the dish, the plate may be used to contact the total surface of the area being sampled.

Estimates of bacterial numbers may be made after gross examination of incubated agar plates. The use of **RODAC® plates** permits the most precise counting of bacterial numbers.

To stop or minimize the transmission of communicable diseases, it is necessary to interrupt the chain of their spread by eliminating the source of microorganisms or at least greatly reducing their numbers. This can be done through **disinfection** of environmental surfaces using **disinfectants** and handwashing with specialized chemicals called **antiseptics**.

EXPERIMENT 1: HOW MICROORGANISMS ARE TRANSMITTED

Objectives

1. Demonstrate how microbes on environmental objects can be transferred to a person and possibly to a group of persons.
2. Demonstrate how microorganisms can be transmitted or transferred directly from one person to another, and possibly to a group of persons.
3. Quantify the number of bacterial cells on living surfaces.

Precautions

1. Wear a disposable apron.
2. Wash your hands with an antimicrobial soap such as liquid Dial® every time you enter or leave the lab.
3. Wipe tabletops thoroughly with Lysol®.
4. Be extremely careful when using the Bunsen burner.
5. Once the inoculating loop is sterilized, do not touch it to table, hands, etc.
6. Avoid contact of bleach with your skin, eyes, and clothing.
7. Discard all materials in biohazard containers for proper disposal.
8. Autoclave ALL materials as soon as you no longer need them.
9. NEVER discard cultures in the trash can.

Materials

1. Ground meat, or a house plant with very moist soil
2. Wooden cutting board
3. Antimicrobial soap
4. China marker

Learning About Microbes

5. Dishwashing soap
6. RODAC® or Trypticase Soy agar (TSA) plates for fingertip colony counts
7. Biohazard bag
8. Masking tape

Procedure (Students A and B, working in pairs.)

Student A

1. Label the bottom of a RODAC® or TSA plate with your initials, the date, and "hand before use." Keep the petri dish cover in place until you are ready to use it.

2. Take a culture sample of the fingertips of your right hand as follows:

   (a) Remove top lid of petri dish.

   (b) Gently press the tips of your five fingers on the surface of the agar for about 15 seconds so that you leave an impression of each tip. Be sure that your fingertips completely touch the agar surface.

   (c) Close the lid and tape it to the base using two small pieces of masking tape.

3. Label the bottom of another agar plate with your initials, the date, and "hand after use."

4. Using both hands, roll food (or soil) on the cutting board. Be sure your fingertips make contact with the food! **Don't allow your hands to touch any other object!**

5. Take a culture sample of fingertips of your right hand, following the described procedure in step 2.

6. Again, roll meat (or plant soil) on cutting board.

7. Using right hands, shake hands with student B after student B completes step 3 in the "Student B" section. Be sure to grip tightly! **Don't allow your hands to touch any other object!**

8. Dispose of meat or soil.

9. Clean the cutting board with antibacterial soap and warm water.

10. Wash your hands well with the antibacterial soap.

Student B

1. Label the bottom of a RODAC® or TSA plate with your initials, the date, and "hand before shake."
2. Take a culture sample of the fingertips of your right hand following the procedure described in step 2 for Student A.
3. Label another agar plate with your initials, the date and "hand" after shake.
4. Shake right hands with Student A, after Student A completes step 6.
5. Following the procedure described in step 2 for Student A, take a culture sample of the fingertips of your right hand used in the handshake with Student A.
6. Wash your hands well with the antimicrobial soap.

Students A and B: Tape plates together with two pieces of masking tape. Incubate all plates in an upside-down position on a window sill at room temperature for at least two days or until bacterial colonies are visible. At end of lab, dispose of plates in biohazard bag.

Observations/Conclusions:

1. Examine the culture plates.
2. Count the number of bacterial colonies on each plate and record your results on Table 1 of the Laboratory Report Form.
3. Compare the "before" and "after" plates.
4. Is there a difference in the number of colonies on the "before" and the "after" plates? If so, what is the significance?

Questions

1. How are bacterial colonies detected and counted?

Learning About Microbes

2. Did all the bacterial colonies look alike? If not, what could account for differences in appearance?

3. Which cultures— "before" or "after"—gave rise to the largest bacterial counts?

4. Did the handshake with student A, who contacted food or soil, spread microbes to student B?

5. If student A, who contacted food or soil, had shaken the hands of students X, Y, and Z (assuming that they have clean, washed hands), and you had taken culture samples of students X, Y and Z's hands after the handshakes, would the bacterial counts of their cultures increase or decrease after the handshakes?

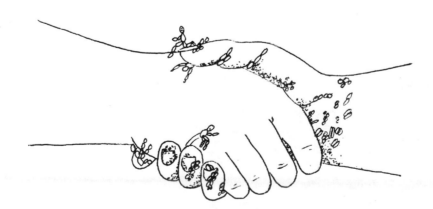

Learning About Microbes

EXPERIMENT 2: TRANSMISSION OF MICROORGANISMS BETWEEN THE ENVIRONMENT AND HUMANS

Objectives

1. Demonstrate how to interrupt the transmission of microorganisms between the environment and people.
2. Demonstrate how to interrupt the transmission of microorganisms between persons.
3. Quantify the numbers of bacterial cells on inanimate surfaces.

The RODAC rhythm

Rock and roll

Materials

1. Ground meat or a house plant with very moist soil
2. Wooden cutting board
3. Antimicrobial soap
4. Household bleach
5. China markers
6. Paper towels
7. Trypticase Soy agar (TSA) plates for fingertip colony counts
8. 3 RODAC® or other TSA plates with colony counting grids (**Hycheck®** paddles) for sampling of cutting board
9. Masking tape
10. Dishwashing soap
11. Biohazard bag

Procedure (Students C and D, working in pairs.)

Student C

1. Label one RODAC® plate with your initials, the date, and "board before use."
2. Take a culture sample of a clean cutting board as follows:

    (a) Remove the lid of the RODAC® petri dish.

(b) Take the bottom lid, containing the mound of culture medium, and roll it on the surface of the board.

(c) Make sure that the entire surface of the agar firmly contacts the sample surface by gently pressing in the bottom of the dish with the knuckles of your second or third finger.

(d) Close the lid and tape it to the base using two small pieces of masking tape.

3. Label a second RODAC® plate with your initials, the date, and "board after use."

4. Using both hands, roll meat (or soil) on the cutting board. Be sure to make complete contact between the food and the cutting board! Wipe hands thoroughly with paper towels!

5. Gently remove the largest amounts of food/soil from the board and dispose of them in biohazard bags.

6. Following the procedure described in step 2, take a sample of the cutting board using the second RODAC® plate.

7. Thoroughly wash the cutting board with dishwashing soap and warm water.

8. Rinse well. Carefully pour bleach on the board and let it stand for 15 minutes. **Take care not to splash bleach on clothes or in eyes!**

9. Wipe the board dry with paper towels.

10. Label the third RODAC® plate with your initials, the date, and "board after wash."

11. Take a culture sample of the cutting board following the procedure described in step 2.

Student D

1. Label one TSA plate with your initials, the date, and "hand before use."

2. Take a culture sample of the fingertips of your right hand using the procedure described in step 2 for Student A.

3. Label another TSA plate with your initials, the date, and "hand after use."

4. Using both hands, roll the food (or soil) on the cutting board. **Be sure to contact your fingertips with the food! Don't allow your hands to touch any other object!**

5. Take a culture sample of the fingertips of your right hand using the procedure followed in step 2.

6. Label another TSA plate with your initials, the date, and "hand after wash."

Learning About Microbes

7. Roll the food (or soil) on the cutting boards. **Don't allow your hands to touch any other object!**

8. Thoroughly wash your hands with antimicrobial soap and warm water.

9. Completely dry your hands with paper towels.

10. Take a culture sample of the fingertips of one of your washed hands.

Students C and D: Tape all plates together with two pieces of masking tape. Incubate all culture plates in an upside-down position at room temperature on a window sill for at least two days or until bacterial colonies are visible. At end of lab, dispose of plates in biohazard bag.

Observations/Conclusions

1. Examine the culture plates.

2. Count the number of bacterial colonies on each plate and record your results on Table 2 of the Laboratory Report Form.

3. Compare the "before use," "after use," and "after wash" plates.

4. Is there a difference in the number of colonies on the plates? If so, what is the significance?

Questions

1. Which cultures gave rise to the largest bacterial counts?

2. Does handwashing with soap contribute to or interfere with the transmission of microbes between persons?

Learning About Microbes

3. Suppose Student X (assuming he/she has clean, washed hands) touches the cutting board after it was used by Student A, but before the cleaning/washing of the board. If you take culture samples of both students' hands before and after they touched the board, would the bacterial counts increase or decrease?

4. Did disinfection of the cutting board contribute to or interfere with the transmission of microbes between persons and the environment?

Key Terms

antiseptic
cholera
contaminated material
disinfectant
disinfection
epidemic

Hycheck®
mucosal surface
RODAC® plate
sewage contamination
source of contamination
vehicle

Learning About Microbes

THE FAR SIDE By GARY LARSON

Working alone, Professor Dawson stumbles
into a bad section of the petri dish.

Suggested Reading

Brock, T. ed. *Milestones in Microbiology*. Prentice-Hall, Englewood Cliffs, NJ, 1975.

Prescott, L.M., and Harley, J.P., Klein, D.A. *Microbiology*. 3rd ed., William C. Brown, Dubuque, IA, 1996.

Tortora, G.J., Funke, B.R., and Case, C.L. *Microbiology —An Introduction*. 6th ed., Benjamin Cummings, Redwood City, CA, 1997.

Learning About Microbes

Microbiology Laboratory Report Form

Name _____ Date _____

Experiment 1

TABLE 1	
STUDENT A	**COLONY COUNT**
Before food or soil	
After food or soil	

STUDENT B	
Before handshake	
After handshake	

Experiment 2

TABLE 2		
STUDENT C	**COLONY COUNT** Board	**COLONY COUNT** Hands
Before use		
After use		
After wash		

STUDENT D	**COLONY COUNT** Board	**COLONY COUNT** Hands
Before use		
After use		
After wash		

TRANSMISSION AND CONTROL OF MICROBES: CONTROLLING MICROBES

- ◆ Grade Level: 10–12
- ◆ Time Required for Experiment: three class periods

EXPERIMENT 1: HANDWASHING

Materials

Prepare the "contaminated object" to be used for plate 2. Using a tube of sterile saline or sterile distilled water, aseptically add a small amount of bakers' yeast until the tube becomes cloudy. Mix the tube thoroughly. Dip a sterile cotton swab in the tube. Use the swab to "contaminate" any convenient object such as a pencil, a key, a rock, or anything that might catch the imagination of the class. Place the "contaminated" object into a sterile petri dish for use by the students. After incubation, the yeast will appear as shiny, off-white, smooth growth on the object. At the conclusion of the experiment, the contaminated object should be soaked overnight in a 5 percent solution of Lysol® (or autoclaved) and then discarded.

Observations/Conclusions

Plate 1: A variety of microorganisms will have developed on the plate where you touched your fingers to the surface. The smaller colonies are probably bacteria and the "fuzzy" colonies are probably fungi.

Plate 2: The growth where your middle finger wiped the surface should be off-white because of the organism used to contaminate the object you touched. These organisms do not cause disease.

Plate 3: You will probably see that wiping your hand with a paper towel did not completely remove all the microbes from your fingers.

Plate 4: If there is significantly less growth on plate 4, then you have shown that washing with antimicrobial soap removes (and kills) microbes effectively.

Answers to Questions

1. Your hands harbor a population of microbes as a result of normal contact with everyday objects. Simply rinsing and wiping your hands does not prevent the transmission of microbes. A more thorough cleansing using antimicrobial soap is required.

2. Unexpected results often occur when performing scientific experiments. In this experiment you may observe bacterial growth on areas of the plate where your fingers did not touch. These microbes might have been introduced as contaminants from the air. You may also observe that the soap did not completely remove all microbes from your fingers; this should tell you that a longer period of washing or a more concentrated soap should be used.

EXPERIMENT 2: EFFECT OF BOILING ON MICROBIAL GROWTH

Observations/Conclusions

Tube 1: should show bacterial growth.

Tube 2: which was inoculated after the contaminated swab had been boiled for 15 minutes, will probably be clear because most bacteria are killed by the heat exposure. Some common airborne bacteria belonging to the genus *Bacillus*, however, form heat-resistant spores that may survive boiling water for 15 minutes. If there is growth in tube 2 you may have picked up this kind of bacteria.

EXPERIMENT 3: COMPARISON OF THE ANTIBACTERIAL EFFECTS OF DIFFERENT SUBSTANCES

Materials

Antibiotics: Can be purchased on small filter paper disks (Difco)

Disinfectants: Prepare dilute solutions of the disinfectants and dip small, sterile filter paper disks into the solution and then aseptically place them onto the agar surface.

Answer to Questions

As molecules of antibiotics and disinfectants or metallic ions from the paper clip diffuse outward from their source and spread through the agar, they may inhibit or kill microbes. You will see this as an area on the plate where no growth occurs, but you cannot tell by looking at the plate whether the organisms were killed or whether their multiplication was simply inhibited.

Some antibiotics and disinfectants are more effective against some kinds of microbes than against others. Since members of the class will probably have picked up different types of organisms when they prepared the plates, not all plates will show the same results.

Key Terms

antibiotic—a microbial product or its derivative that kills susceptible microorganisms or inhibits their growth

antiseptic—an antimicrobial substance that can be applied to body surfaces

aseptic—absence of contamination by unwanted microorganisms

commensalism—system of interaction in which two organisms live in association with one another; one benefits, and the other neither benefits nor is harmed

disinfectant—a chemical, often toxic, used on inanimate objects to kill vegetative forms of microorganisms

inoculate—introduce microorganisms into a culture medium or host

lawn—confluent growth of bacteria on an agar surface

microbe—any of the bacteria, protozoa, viruses, or various fungi and algae

mutualism—a relationship between two organisms in which both organisms benefit

osmotic pressure—the force exerted by substances dissolved in a solution on a membrane they cannot penetrate

parasitism—a relationship between two organisms in which one benefits (parasite) at the expense of another (host)

pathogen—disease-causing microbe

pH—a representation of the alkalinity or acidity of a substance

ubiquitous—widespread

Controlling Microbes

INTRODUCTION

Microbes, organisms too small to be seen with the naked eye, are all around us. They are in the air we breathe, the water we drink, and the ground we walk upon. Microbes are also in—and on—our bodies. The microbes exist in a **parasitic**, **mutualistic**, or **commensal** relationship with the human body, which acts as a host. Usually, these **ubiquitous** microorganisms are harmless. When an individual has an infectious disease, however, it is important that the transmission of the **pathogenic** microbes be halted. Various food industries, pharmaceutical manufacturers, water treatment plants, health care facilities, and many other concerns constantly monitor for the presence of microbes and maintain quality by controlling the microbes in their respective environments.

There are various ways to control microorganisms. Physical means to do so include irradiation (ultraviolet and gamma), extremes of **osmotic pressure** and **pH**, and heat. **Disinfectants**, **antiseptics**, and **antibiotics** are chemical means to control microbes. Discuss with your classmates the various ways to control microbes before performing these exercises.

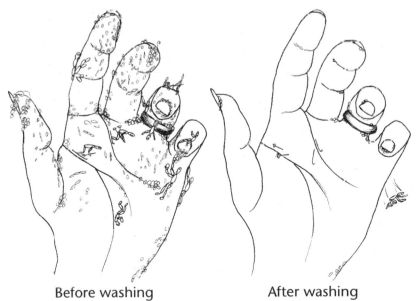

Before washing   After washing

Objectives

1. Examine the effectiveness of hand soap, boiling, antibiotics, and disinfectants in the control of microbial growth.
2. Determine if your hands may be the source of microbes for this study.

EXPERIMENT 1: HANDWASHING

Materials

1. Antimicrobial soap
2. Paper towels
3. China marker
4. Nutrient agar plates [4 per student]
5. Contaminated objects*
6. Biohazard bag
7. Masking tape

Procedure

IMPORTANT: DO NOT wash your hands before you begin today's work.

1. Mark the bottom of each Nutrient agar plate with your initials and the date and number the plates 1 through 4.
2. Plate 1—Open the lid of the petri plate like a clamshell, just enough to insert your fingers. Gently touch the center of the plate with the three middle fingers of your unwashed left hand.
3. Plate 2—Open the lid of the petri plate like a clamshell, just enough to insert your fingers. Using *only* the middle finger of your left hand, touch the contaminated object. Now gently touch the center of plate 2 with all *three middle fingers* of your left hand.
4. Plate 3—Wipe your left hand with a paper towel. Open the lid of the petri plate like a clamshell, just enough to insert your fingers. Gently touch all three middle fingers of your left hand to the center of the plate.

---

* See your instructor.

Learning About Microbes

5. Plate 4—Wash your hands thoroughly with antimicrobial soap and warm water. Dry both hands with a clean paper towel. Open the lid of the petri plate like a clamshell, just enough to insert your fingers. Gently touch the three middle fingers of the your left hand to the center of plate 4.

6. Tape the four plates together and turn them upside down. Store plates at room temperature until the next class period (or incubate at 37°C for 48 hours). Your instructor should include an uninoculated Nutrient agar plate as a control.

7. Record results in Table 1 of the Laboratory Report form.

8. Save one of the four plates that has an isolated colony for use in Experiment 2.

Observations/Conclusions

1. Plate 1: What evidence do you see that there were microbes on your fingers?

2. Plate 2: Is there anything special about the area where your middle finger touched the agar surface?

3. Plate 3: Did wiping your hand with a paper towel have any effect on the presence of microbes?

4. Plate 4: What effect did handwashing with antimicrobial soap have on the microbes on your hands?

Questions

1. What does this experiment tell you about handwashing?

2. Did anything occur on any of the four plates that did not seem right? If so, describe it and try to explain it.

EXPERIMENT 2: EFFECT OF BOILING ON MICROBIAL GROWTH

Materials

1. China marker
2. Sterile swabs
3. Forceps
4. Test tube rack
5. Sterile Nutrient broth tube [2 per student]
6. Nutrient agar plate [1 per student]
7. Boiling water bath (1L beaker with boiling water heated by Bunsen burner)
8. Plate from Experiment 1
9. Biohazard bag

Procedure

1. Mark both Nutrient broth tubes with your initials and date. Label them #1 and #2. Keep them in the test-tube rack.

2. Mark the bottom of a Nutrient agar plate with your initials and the date. Draw a line dividing the plate in half and label one side "A" and the other side "B."

3. Choose an isolated colony from the Experiment 1 plate. Circle the colony on the bottom of the plate with a marker and record details of its appearance on Table 2 of the Laboratory Report Form.

4. Touch the tip of a sterile swab to the isolated colony from Experiment 1, picking up as much of the colony as possible.

5. **Aseptically inoculate** broth tube #1 by inserting the swab and twirling it in the tube to dislodge as many bacteria as possible.

6. Press the swab against the inside of the tube to remove excess broth. Remove the swab from the tube and replace the cap on the broth tube. Continue to hold the swab handle in your hand; **DO NOT** lay it down! Put the tube in the test tube rack.

7. Using the swab from the previous step, aseptically inoculate the Nutrient agar plate so that the entire surface of the plate is covered, rotating the plate between applications to form a **lawn**. See diagram below. Replace the lid. Set this plate aside for Experiment 3.

Preparation of Lawn of Bacteria

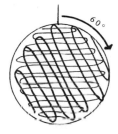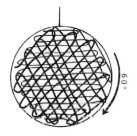

8. Place the swab in a boiling water bath for 15 minutes.

9. Remove the swab with forceps and aseptically transfer it to tube 2. Break off the upper half of the swab, leaving the bottom half in tube 2. Replace the cap on the broth tube.

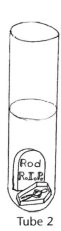

Tube 1   Tube 2

10. Store the newly inoculated tubes in the test tube rack at room temperature until the next class period (or incubate at 37°C for 48 hours). Your instructor should include sterile Nutrient broth tubes as controls.

Learning About Microbes

Observations/Conclusions

1. Is tube 1 cloudy or clear? Is tube 2 cloudy or clear?

2. When you put the swab into tube 1, did it have living bacteria on it?

3. Did the bacteria grow in tube 1? How do you know?

4. When you put the swab into tube 2, did it have living bacteria on it?

5. Did the bacteria grow in tube 2? How do you know?

6. Record details of the isolated colony's appearance on Table 2 of the Laboratory Report form.

Questions

1. What does this experiment reveal about the effect of boiling water on bacteria?

2. Did anything occur in the broth tubes that did not seem right? If so, describe it and try to explain it.

EXPERIMENT 3: COMPARISON OF THE ANTIBACTERIAL EFFECTS OF DIFFERENT SUBSTANCES

Materials

1. Metal paper clips
2. Plastic or plastic-coated paper clips
3. Penicillin disks
4. Kanamycin disks
5. Lysol®
6. Household bleach (Clorox®)
7. Forceps
8. Agar plate with lawn of bacteria from Experiment 2
9. Bunsen burner
10. Masking tape
11. Biohazard bag
12. Beakers of ethyl alcohol
13. Sterile filter paper disks

Procedure

1. Choose one of the following pairs (A and B of same item) of test substances for use on the lawn plate prepared in Experiment 2.

Item	A	B
paper clip	metal	plastic or plastic-coated
antibiotic*	penicillin	kanamycin
disinfectant*	Lysol®	household bleach

2. Using flame-sterilized forceps (your teacher will demonstrate), place the "A" unit of your pair in the center of the "A" side of the lawn plate. Tap the object lightly so that it adheres to the agar surface.

3. Reflame the forceps and allow them to cool for a few seconds.

4. Using the flame-sterilized forceps, place the "B" unit of your pair in the center of the "B" side of the lawn plate. Tap the object lightly so that it adheres to the agar surface.

5. Using two small pieces of masking tape, tape the plates together and incubate in an upside-down position at room temperature until the next class period (or incubate at 37°C for 48 hours).

---

* See your instructor.

Learning About Microbes

Observations/Conclusions

1. Did bacteria grow to the edge of object A?

2. Did bacteria grow to the edge of object B?

3. What does a zone of "no growth" around one of the test objects mean?

4. Use Table 3 to record results from plates inoculated by the other students.

Questions

1. What do the data tell you about the effects of heavy metal ions on bacteria?

2. What do the data tell you about the effects of different antibiotics on bacteria?

3. What do the data tell you about the effects of different disinfectants on bacteria?

Key Terms

antibiotic
antiseptic
aseptic
commensalism
disinfectant
inoculate
lawn

microbe
mutualism
osmotic pressure
parasitism
pathogen
pH
ubiquitous

Suggested Readings

Prescott, L.M., Harley J.P., and Klein, D. A. *Microbiology*. 3rd ed., William C. Brown, Dubuque, IA, 1996.

Seeley, H. W., Jr., Vandemark, P. J., and Lee, J. J. *Microbes in Action*. W. H. Freeman, New York, NY, 1990.

Learning About Microbes

Microbiology Laboratory Report Form

Name _____ Date _____

TABLE 1	
PLATE NUMBER	**RESULTS**
1	
2	
3	
4	

TABLE 2

Circle one word from each column that best describes the colony. Describe the color.

SIZE OF COLONY	COLOR	CONSISTENCY
Big		Dry
Medium		Wet
Small		Shiny
Very small		Gummy

TABLE 3

TEST OBJECT	NUMBER OF PLATES WITH ZONES OF NO GROWTH	TOTAL NUMBER OF PLATES
Metal paper clip		
Plastic paper clip		
Penicillin		
Kanamycin		
Lysol®		
Household bleach (Clorox®)		

Microbial Genetics

MICROBIAL GENETICS

◆ **Grade Level:** 10–12, college
◆ **Time Required for Experiment:** one class period; daily observations for five to seven days

EXPERIMENT 1: MODIFICATION

Materials

Grow the *S. marcescens* in 10 ml of Nutrient broth at 25°C for 48 hours.

Observations

Growth should be best at 37°C but the vivid red color should be best at 25°C (room temperature).

Answers to Questions

1. A modification is a *temporary* change that might be due to a change in growth conditions and metabolism, as observed in this experiment. Since a mutation is a genetic change (a change in the DNA), the change in incubation temperatures would have little or no effect.

2. To prove a modification had taken place, you could transfer growth from tubes showing pigmentation to fresh culture media. Cultures of tubes *without* the red color would also be transferred to fresh media. Both sets of new inoculations would then be incubated at each temperature used in this experiment.

If the results are the same as previously observed (pigmentation is best at room temperature and little or no pigmentation is observed at other temperatures), then a modification has taken place.

EXPERIMENT 2: MUTATION

Answers to Questions

1. You could incubate these cultures at different temperatures as in the modification experiment. If a mutation has occurred, a permanent change has taken place in the cultures. Although the cultures will grow, they will *not* produce the red pigment at room temperature.

2. To produce a mutation, an agent (in this case, UV light) is used to bring about a genetic change. Most of these changes are lethal (that is, they cause death). Some organisms in the experiment did survive even though their genetic composition had been altered.

3. Examples include air sterilization in a doctor's office or hospital, water sterilization in small containers (such as a thermos), and sterilization of surfaces used for transfer of microorganisms (such as lab bench tops).

Key Terms

allele—a member of a pair of genes controlling a particular trait

antibiotic—a microbial product or its derivative that kills susceptible microorganisms or inhibits their growth

binary fission—the act of splitting into two; a form of asexual reproduction

chromosome—a rod-shaped or circular mass of DNA that carries hereditary characteristics

complementary strand—one of two strands making the double helix of DNA

DNA—abbreviation for deoxyribonucleic acid; chemical substance that makes up the genetic material of all cells

dominant—the appearance of one of two mutually antagonistic parental characteristics

gene—a unit of heredity

hydrogen bond—a weak attraction between a hydrogen atom covalently bonded to nitrogen or oxygen and another covalently bonded to nitrogen or oxygen

lawn—confluent growth of bacteria on an agar surface

modification—a temporary change in the form or characteristics of an organism

mutation—a process in which a gene undergoes a permanent structural change

nucleotide—a class of compounds consisting of a carbohydrate (sugar), a purine or pyrimidine base, and a phosphate group

procaryotes—a group of organisms characterized by lack of a nuclear membrane and organelles in the cell

recessive—an allele that is expressed only when the gene is carried by both chromosomes

ultraviolet light—atoms that travel at a wavelength of 13.46 to 400nm; radiation of these wavelengths are most harmful to microorganisms

Microbial Genetics

INTRODUCTION

Genetics is the study of how organisms resemble their parents. It is one of the newest biological sciences, beginning just over 100 years ago with the studies of the Austrian monk Gregor Mendel. His work involved observations, tests, hypotheses, and numerical analyses of the growth and appearance of peas. To explain his findings he defined the unit responsible for a single trait as a **gene**. In addition, Mendel established that this unit of inheritance, the gene, might exist in one or more varieties called an **allele.**

In the early 1900's, T. H. Morgan studied the genetics of the fruit fly *Drosophila melanogaster*. While observing these flies, he noted that some characteristics are **dominant** and others are **recessive**. Morgan discovered two phenomena: **mutation**, which is a permanent change in characteristics, and **modification**, which is a temporary change in characteristics. Even after these significant finds, for nearly three decades little progress was made in understanding how microbial characteristics are inherited. The advent of **antibiotics**, and the development of resistance to them by some microorganisms, led to the discovery that bacteria exhibit much the same genetic characteristics as more advanced organisms. A series of experiments by Watson and Crick culminated in a report in 1953 in which they described the chemical structure of **DNA** and announced that genetic information resides in the **nucleotide** sequence of the DNA.

In **procaryotes**, which do not have a true nucleus, a **chromosome** is a threadlike molecule of DNA. The molecule is a double chain of nucleotides arranged in a helix with the nucleotide base pairs held together by **hydrogen bonds**. The typical procaryotic cell contains a single circular chromosome composed of double-stranded DNA. When a procaryotic cell reproduces by **binary fission**, the chromosome reproduces itself; each single strand of the DNA makes a **complementary strand** that is a copy of itself.

Objectives

1. Demonstrate mutation and modification in microorganisms.
2. Observe the effects of **ultraviolet (UV) light** on microorganisms.

Precautions

1. Handle the bacterial cultures with care. Wash your hands with antimicrobial soap before and after handling cultures, and wash work surfaces with disinfectant.
2. Clean up spills using disposable plastic gloves, paper towels, and disinfectant. Dispose of all cleanup materials in the biohazard bag.
3. Do not put fingers or any objects near eyes or mouth while working.
4. Do not expose skin or eyes directly to the UV lamp. Wear special protective UV goggles and plastic gloves.

Designer genes

EXPERIMENT 1: MODIFICATION

Objectives

1. Demonstrate that a change in characteristics is not always the result of a genetic change.
2. Determine if changes in characteristics are due to the environmental conditions in which the organisms are grown.
3. Determine the validity of findings when recording genetic observations.
4. Learn the technique for making a **lawn** of bacteria.

Materials

1. Nutrient broth culture of *Serratia marcescens* grown at 25°C for 48 hours
2. Nutrient agar plates [4]
3. Sterile cotton swabs [4]
4. China markers
5. Refrigerator
6. Incubator set at 37°C
7. Incubator set at 55°C
8. Masking tape
9. Disposal beaker of disinfectant
10. Biohazard bag

Procedure

1. Label the bottom of each petri dish with your initials and the date. Also label each plate with one of the incubation temperatures:

   5°C = Refrigerator
   25°C = Room temperature
   37°C = Body temperature
   55°C = High temperature

2. Aseptically place a sterile swab into the broth culture of *S. marcescens*. Twirl the swab to saturate the cotton and then press the swab against the side of the tube to squeeze out any excess fluid.

3. Open one of the petri dishes like a clamshell and completely streak the surface of the nutrient agar with the inoculated swab. See diagram below.

Starting a lawn of bacteria

4. Close the lid, rotate the plate, and streak again. Repeat this procedure at least two more times to ensure that the surface is completely covered and will grow as a lawn of bacteria. See diagrams below.

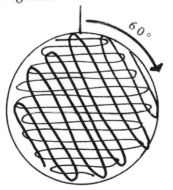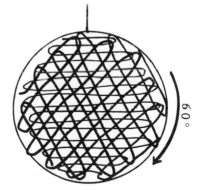

Completing a lawn of bacteria

Learning About Microbes

5. Replace the lid and, using a new sterile swab for each plate, repeat this process for the three remaining petri plates. Dispose of used swabs in the beaker of disinfectant or as instructed.

6. Using two pieces of tape, secure the lids to the bases of the inoculated petri plates.

7. Turn the plates upside down and incubate each one at the proper temperature.

8. Observe the amount of growth and the color produced at 24-hour intervals for 5 days.

Observations

1. Record the results in Table 1 on the Laboratory Report Form.

2. Determine the temperature at which the most growth occurred.

Questions

1. How does this procedure demonstrate that a modification, not a mutation, has taken place?

2. What alterations would you make to this procedure to prove that a modification occurred?

EXPERIMENT 2: MUTATION

Objectives

1. Observe how ultraviolet light permanently affects microorganisms.

2. Determine the effectiveness of different materials in blocking ultraviolet light.

3. Learn the correct and safe usage of ultraviolet light in the laboratory.

Materials

1. Broth culture of *Serratia marcescens*
2. Shortwave ultraviolet lamp [(2537 A)- Sterilamp®]
3. Masking tape
4. Nutrient agar (NA) plates [3]
5. Sterile swabs
6. China marker
7. UV goggles
8. Protective gloves
9. 25°C incubator (optional)
10. Biohazard bag

Procedure

1. Label the three Nutrient agar plates with your initials and the date. Label each plate as to the treatment it will undergo.

    Plate 1: UV Exposure—Lid Off
    Plate 2: UV Exposure—Lid On
    Plate 3: Control

2. Using a sterile swab, aseptically streak the broth culture over the surface of the three Nutrient agar plates, covering the agar surface entirely to make a lawn, as done in Experiment 1.

3. Prewarm the short wavelength ultraviolet (UV) lamp for at least 10 minutes. Use protective gloves and UV goggles and **do not look directly at the light.** Place plate 1 under the lamp and remove the lid. Tilt the plate slightly from side to side to allow for uniform exposure. Expose the plate for 2 minutes. The distance from the lamp to the culture should be approximately 12 inches.

4. Repeat the UV exposure with plate 2, leaving the lid in place. Expose this plate for 2 minutes also.

5. Do not expose plate 3 to the UV light.

6. Tape all three plates together and incubate them upside down at room temperature and in a dark place for 72 hours (in a 25°C incubator if possible).

Observations

Record the appearance of the three plates in Table 2 of the Laboratory Report Form.

Questions

1. How would you prove that a mutation has occurred?

2. Did UV light affect the number of organisms that grew? Why or why not?

3. Can you think of a practical use of UV light as a deterrent to microbial growth?

Key Terms

allele
antibiotic
binary fission
chromosome
complementary strand
DNA
dominant
gene

hydrogen bond
lawn
modification
mutation
nucleotide
procaryotes
recessive
ultraviolet light

Suggested Reading

Campbell, N. A. *Biology.* Benjamin Cummings, Menlo Park, CA, 1987.

Learning About Microbes

Microbiology Laboratory Report Form

Name _____ Date _____

Describe the color of the growth in the column marked "C."

Use the following key to describe the amount of growth in the column marked "A":

no growth = –   moderate growth = ++

slight growth = +   abundant growth = +++

TABLE 1—Modification										
TEMPERATURE	DAY 1		DAY 2		DAY 3		DAY 4		DAY 5	
	C	A	C	A	C	A	C	A	C	A
5°C										
25°C										
37°C										
55°C										

Describe the color of the growth in the column marked "Color."

Use the following key to describe the amount of growth in the column marked "Amount of Growth":

no growth = –   moderate growth = ++

slight growth = +   abundant growth = +++

TABLE 2—Mutation		
PLATE	COLOR	AMOUNT OF GROWTH
Plate 1		
Plate 2		
Plate 3		

Motility: Dynamics of
Growth in the Microbial World

MOTILITY: DYNAMICS OF GROWTH IN THE MICROBIAL WORLD

◆ Grade Level: 7–12, college
◆ Time Required for Experiment: one class period for discussion and inoculation; one class period for observations

EXPERIMENT 1: SWARMING MOTILITY

Materials

The plate cultures of *Proteus mirabilis* may be prepared by inoculating plates of Trypticase Soy agar and incubating overnight at 37°C.

Answers to Questions

1. The motility is random. However, the observed swarming is always toward a fresh supply of food. This involves a movement away from the original point of inoculation, which creates an outward, circular pattern.

2. The ability to swarm is an inherent property of only some bacteria. Therefore, the presence or absence of swarming may be used as a factor in the identification of bacteria.

EXPERIMENT 2: STAB TECHNIQUE

Materials

Broth cultures of each organism may be prepared by inoculating tubes of Trypticase Soy broth with the appropriate culture and incubating overnight at 37°C.

Answers to Questions

1. The *S. marcescens* culture should have been motile. After incubation, growth away from the line of inoculation in the stab is indicated by an increased cloudiness or a turbid appearance.

2. Bacteria that grew at their optimum growth temperature should have exhibited more motility.

3. At their optimum growth temperature, bacteria are more active physically and metabolically. Therefore, you will observe more motility under these conditions.

Key Terms

bacillus—a rod-shaped bacterium

Enterobacteriaceae—a family of gram-negative bacilli, commonly found in the intestinal tract of man and other animals, that are active fermenters of glucose and other carbohydrates

flagella—thin, hairlike appendages that propel bacteria and some larger microorganisms

gram-negative—bacteria that stain pink or red after the Gram stain. The bacterial walls are composed of a peptidoglycan layer surrounded by a lipopolysaccharide outer membrane.

motility—the ability of an organism to move by itself

opportunistic pathogen—an organism that does not ordinarily cause a disease but can become pathogenic (i.e. cause disease) under certain circumstances

optimum temperature—the temperature at which a given species grows best

peritrichous—having flagella distributed over the entire cell

semisolid agar—partially solid culture medium made by the addition of a lower percentage of agar than is used for a totally solid agar. It has the consistency of Jell-O® that is not yet set and allows for the movement of motile organisms within the agar itself.

septation—a cross wall between cells

stab—a culture medium that results when molten agar is poured into a test tube and allowed to harden with the tube in an upright position

swarming—the phenomenon exhibited by certain actively motile organisms in which they are able to rapidly spread over the surface of a moist agar plate. A feature of this activity is its periodicity: it occurs in successive waves, separated by periods of growth and cell division.

swimmer—the term used to describe a motile cell with extra flagella

turbid—having a cloudy appearance

Motility: Dynamics of Growth in the Microbial World

INTRODUCTION

Various microorganisms have the ability to propel themselves. This characteristic is termed **motility**. Motility is not necessary for survival. It can, however, provide the microbe with advantages. Motility may allow the microbe to move toward a more favorable environment, as in the search for nutrients. It may also allow the microbe to flee from an adverse environment, such as when a predator is nearby.

Motility in bacteria, if present, is accomplished by means of hair-like appendages called **flagella**. These structures are composed of a single protein, flagellin. To visualize flagella under the light microscope is extremely difficult, if not impossible, unless a special staining procedure is used. However, there are indirect means of demonstrating the presence of flagella as described in the following experiments.

Some bacteria exhibit "swarming" motility, where the growth of the bacteria appears as waves on the agar. One of the most active bacteria that exhibits this type of motility is the rod-shaped organism, *Proteus mirabilis*. It is a **gram-negative bacillus**, similar to many of the other **Enterobacteriaceae**. It is normally harmless but may be considered an **opportunistic pathogen** and is sometimes associated with urinary tract infections.

When this species of bacteria is grown in a broth culture medium, it forms **peritrichous** flagella (flagella distributed evenly around the entire cell surface). However, when the organisms are grown on a culture medium solidified by agar, a change in cellular morphology takes place. The *P. mirabilis* cells elongate to many times their original length with little change in width. After some time, the elongated cells form **septations** and the cells divide, forming a microcolony. These newly formed **swimmer** cells have more flagella than the original cells, enabling them to move over a solid medium by a process called **swarming**. The swarming cannot be accomplished by individual cells. The process requires a coordinated effort of differentiated cells. It will occur when a group of the differentiated swarmer cells moves away from the central area of the medium. The swarming continues until the number of cells in the swarm is reduced as a result of some cells being left behind on the agar's surface. At this point, the swarmer cells revert back to swimmer cells and the process is repeated. Macroscopically (using the naked eye) the growth of *P. mirabilis* on agar will have a wavelike appearance.

Another indirect method of determining if bacteria have flagella is to use a "stab" technique. This technique uses a **semisolid agar** medium that allows the bacteria to move within the agar rather than just on the surface. It is one of the better means of determining the presence or absence of motility when a pathogenic organism is involved because the potential contact with the pathogen by the tester is greatly reduced. The technique involves a straight-line inoculation of the microbe into the depths (3 to 4 cm) of a semisolid agar medium which makes up the stab. After the tube is incubated for 24 to 48 hours at the bacterium's **optimum temperature** for growth, the tube is examined to determine if the organism's growth has spread away from the original line of inoculation. If the organism is highly motile, the incubated tube may have a **turbid** or cloudy appearance.

Objectives

1. Learn the techniques for tests of bacterial motility.
2. Observe various types of bacterial motility.

Precautions

1. Keep all flammable materials away from the flame of the Bunsen burner.
2. Wash your hands before and after lab with an antimicrobial soap.

EXPERIMENT 1: SWARMING MOTILITY

Materials (Work individually or in pairs.)

1. Plate culture of *Proteus mirabilis*
2. Inoculating loop
3. Sterile Nutrient agar plate
4. Bunsen burner
5. China marker
6. Biohazard bag
7. 37°C incubator
8. Masking tape

Learning About Microbes

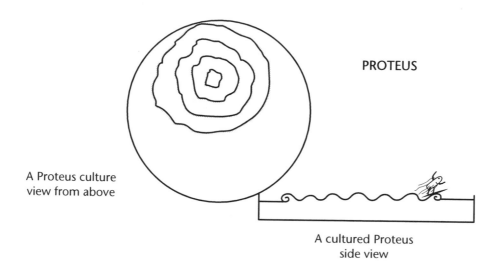

PROTEUS

A Proteus culture
view from above

A cultured Proteus
side view

Procedure

1. Write your name, the date, and the name of the bacteria on the bottom of the Nutrient agar plate.
2. Sterilize the loop by heating it to redness in the Bunsen burner. Then let it cool.
3. Aseptically pick up some of the *P. mirabilis* with the loop.
4. Opening the agar plate like a clamshell, inoculate the center area with the bacteria.
5. Using two small pieces of masking tape, tape the plate closed and incubate in an upside-down position at 37°C for 24 to 48 hours.
6. If the waves of growth are not seen at 48 hours, reincubate the plates for another 24 to 48 hours.

Observations/Conclusions

In the space provided below, sketch the macroscopic appearance of *P. mirabilis* after incubation.

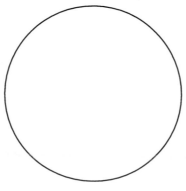

Learning About Microbes

Questions

1. Is the swarming of the bacteria directional or random?

2. How does this swarming help to identify bacteria?

EXPERIMENT 2: STAB TECHNIQUE

Materials (Work individually or in pairs.)

1. Sterile semisolid Nutrient agar stab tubes [2]
2. Culture of *Serratia marcescens*
3. Culture of *Micrococcus luteus*
4. Inoculating wire or needle
5. Bunsen burner
6. China marker
7. Biohazard bag
8. Test-tube rack

Procedure

1. Label each stab tube with your name, the date, and the name of one of the two test bacteria.
2. Flame-sterilize the inoculating wire by heating it to redness in the Bunsen burner, then allow it to cool.
3. Using the wire, aseptically transfer *S. marcescens* to the corresponding uninoculated semisolid stab tube by passing the wire straight down into the agar and pulling it straight back out. See illustration on page 130.

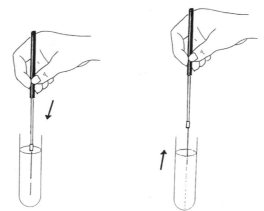

4. Flame-sterilize the wire by heating it to redness again, then allow it to cool.

5. Repeat the inoculation procedure using *M. luteus* and the second stab tube.

6. Place the tubes upright in a test tube rack.

7. One half of the class should incubate their tubes at room temperature for 24 to 48 hours while the other half of the class should incubate their tubes at 37°C for 24 to 48 hours.

8. Your instructor will include semisolid stabs that have been inoculated with a sterile needle to serve as a control.

Observations/Conclusions

In the spaces provided, sketch the appearance of your cultures and the control after incubation. Draw and label the lines of inoculation and write the names of the test bacteria.

Organism: _____   Organism: _____   Control: _____

Temperature: _____   Temperature: _____   Temperature: _____

Learning About Microbes

Questions

1. Which of your cultures showed evidence of motility?

2. Compare your results with those from another student who incubated the cultures at a different temperature. Is there any difference in the motility of the bacteria based on the different temperatures? Why?

3. What do you conclude about the relationship between motility and temperature?

Key Terms

bacillus
Enterobacteriaceae
flagella
gram-negative
motility
opportunistic pathogen
optimum temperature

peritrichous
semisolid agar
septation
stab
swarming
swimmer
turbid

Suggested Readings

Campbell, N. A. *Biology.* Benjamin Cummings, Menlo Park, CA, 1987.

Tortora, G. J., Funke, B. R., and Case, C. L. *Microbiology.* 6th ed., Benjamin Cummings, Menlo Park, CA, 1997.

APPENDIX

Laboratory suppliers of microbiology items including media (partial listing)

Carolina Biological Supply Co.
2700 York Road
Burlington, NC 27215

Fisher Scientific
585 Alpha Drive
Pittsburgh, PA 15238

Wards Natural Science
5100 West Henrietta Road
P.O. Box 92912
Rochester, NY 14692-9012

Materials

5% Lysol®
antimicrobial soap such as Dial® (other brands of antibacterial soap are satisfactory)
beakers (50ml, 200ml, 500ml, 1L)
bibulous paper
biohazard bags such as Fisher Cat No. 01-815C
bleach such as Clorox®
Bunsen burners and gas supply[1]
china marker
compound microscope with 10X, 40X objectives (100X if possible)
cotton swabs (sterile)
culture media
dyes (methylene blue)
emergency eye wash station
ethanol [ethyl alcohol]
eye protection[2]
fire extinguisher
forceps

---

[1] If a gas supply is not available, sterile, disposable loops/needles should be used. Alcohol burners are NOT an acceptable substitute.

[2] It is **strongly** recommended that students perform laboratory work using safety glasses or goggles.

glass microscope slides
glass coverslips
incubators
inoculating loops
inoculating needles
lens paper
masking tape
paper disks (sterile)
paper towels
Pasteur pipets
petri dishes (sterile)
plastic soda bottles
refrigerator
scissors
soil
stains [Gram stain series (crystal violet, safranine, iodine)]
test-tube racks
test tubes
tubes of sterile water

Notes Regarding Materials

Special supplies for experiments found in section on: Interruption of the Transmission of Microorganisms (see page 85).

Prepared plates with trypticase soy agar:
Wards Cat. No. 88W0925
Carolina Cat. No. 82-2020

trypticase soy agar: Wards Cat. No. 88W1815

RODAC® plates may be filled with 12 ml of Trypticase Soy agar.
RODAC® plates: Falcon Plastics Cat. No. 1034, Fisher Scientific Cat. No. 08-757-152
Prepared RODAC® plates with trypticase soy agar: Carolina Cat. No. 82-3000

Hycheck® paddles may serve as an alternative to RODAC® plates: Difco Cat. No. 9053-36-5